To Have Not

A Memoir

By Frances Lefkowitz

To Have Not

A Memoir

By Frances Lefkowitz

MACADAM CAGE

MacAdam/Cage Publishing
155 Sansome Street, Suite 550
San Francisco, CA 94104

www.MacAdamCage.com

Library of Congress Cataloging-in-Publication Data

Lefkowitz, Frances.
 To have not : a memoir / by Frances Lefkowitz.
    p. cm.
 ISBN 978-1-59692-354-6
1. Lefkowitz, Frances. 2. Authors, American—21st century—Biography.
I. Title.
 PS3612.E34975Z46 2009
 813'.6—dc22
 [B]
                            2009028911

AUTHOR'S NOTE: I have tried as hard as I could to tell the truth and still tell
a good story. I am sorry if I got anything wrong or said anything hurtful.
I have avoided names to protect some semblance of privacy. I hope I have
not embarrassed anyone other than myself.

Printed in the United States of America

10 9 8 7 6 5 4 3 2 1

Book and cover design by Dorothy Carico Smith

To my brothers and my parents,
with love, gratitude,
and apologies

TO HAVE NOT

Dos linages solos hay en el mundo,
que son el tener y el no tener
There are only two families in the world,
the haves and the have nots
—Cervantes, *Don Quixote*

Not Heaven itself upon the past has power
—Dryden, *Imitations of Horace*

Prologue
When Poverty Becomes Poison

When us kids used to walk down 16th Street to the schoolyard or across Sanchez to the corner store, we'd keep a lookout for cool cars. When one drove by—a red mustang convertible, a tiny MG, a black Jag with the silver cat ready to pounce off the hood—whoever saw it first would point and say, "That's my car!" We could play this game anywhere, my brothers and their buddies and I, shouting the words loud and fast to drown out anyone else who might be thinking about claiming the same car. You could even play it alone, whispering the three magic words while walking home from school or sitting in a window seat on the bus, leaning your drowsy head against the sun-warmed glass. Then the car would speed off through the traffic, carrying your dreams out of sight. You'd covet, grasp, and lose, all in a few quick seconds of shiny colored metal whizzing by.

But time, like traffic, moves on. In a moment that lasts maybe a year or two, everything that was clear about the world becomes hazy and then sharpens up again, like the view through a camera lens as you twist the focus in and out. What you once knew without thinking begins to clash with the evidence darting out at you from all around, from TV and movies and comic books and magazines and even real life, like the way your mother oversmiles as she takes the crumpled green bills out of her fabric wallet and hands them to the department-store clerk to pay for the book, scarf, dress, hat, and kerchief that you need to join the Brownies. This is the moment when you discover that there are people out there who have things that you don't. You're not sure *why* things are different for those other people, but you are sure *how* they are different: these people have lots of things—new things, big things—and they are always getting more things, and even the things they throw out are things you wouldn't mind having. Now that you know this, it is hard to make a game out of claiming cool cars as your own. And no one—not even your father who finds you melancholy in front of Saturday-morning cartoons—can comfort you, because they have long known and therefore can no longer understand the awfulness of these truths: the world goes on without you, and parts of this life are untouchable.

I have nothing to say about the politics of poverty, what causes it and what it causes and how to make it go away. I can only tell you what poverty does to a person, and how to have not. It gets inside you, nestles into your bones and gives you a chill that you cannot shake. Poverty becomes you—it shapes what you see and taste and dream—till there is no telling where you stop and your poverty begins. To be poor is to live in denial—not the denial of professional counselors and self-help books, which is really an avoidance of some truth too painful to admit, but denial in its most literal sense: you must say no to yourself constantly. Being poor means stripping down to the essentials, and there's not much a person really needs to survive—bread, cheese, blankets, a little black-and-white TV, some toothpaste, soap, pencils, and a library card. In and of itself, it isn't bad to not have things, and if all of us lived this way, there would hardly be anything wrong with it at all. To be poor is one problem; to *know* that you are poor is another problem altogether. That is when poverty becomes poison.

You don't have to be poor to live in poverty, but it helps. That's because poverty is not only a lack of money; it can also be a lack of love or choice, pleasure or safety, faith or confidence or possibility. It seeps into your very cells and makes you believe you are not entitled to have the things that other people have; you are not even allowed to want them, except, sometimes, in your dreams.

Chapter 1
Start With Parents Who Marry by Accident

It wasn't until I was seven, eight, and nine years old and we lived on the corner of 16th and Sanchez that I knew, from TV and movies, from snatches of conversation, from those fancy cars that sometimes drove down our street, that there were things we did not have. Before 16th and Sanchez, we lived on Norwich Street at the other end of San Francisco's Spanish-speaking Mission district. Before that was our first stint in campus housing at San Francisco State on the foggy edge of the city; and before that we lived off Haight Street near the panhandle of Golden Gate Park, where I was born. And somewhere in between these places we spent a few months in a spare room at the apartment of a friend of my father's. This friend, like most people my father knew, was an artist, though I'm not sure how he made his living. He had short, pale hair and a soft voice and wore a wrinkled, butter-colored shirt with a collar; he smoked cigarettes and was quiet and uneasy around children, though he seemed glad to have my brothers and me there, swinging like gibbons from the exposed ceiling pipes in the basement room.

His apartment was half-residential, half-industrial, on the border between three low-rent neighborhoods. Adjacent to our room was a shop filled with power tools, and to walk through there was to walk through a forest, large metal machines looming like pines or even redwoods, coated in layers of curly blond wood shavings. Several years after we stayed with him, he hung himself from those ceiling pipes.

My first memory is from the house on Norwich, up against a rocky hill, several flights of concrete steps from the sidewalk: I am eating lunch in the bathtub, a parsley sandwich floating on a pie tin alongside me. The landlady, who lived in a little house just in front of ours, had planted parsley and a few flowers in the space between her back door and our front door; my mother must have picked some sprigs and stuck them with mayonnaise between two slices of bread. Like all memories, this one, of a girl, maybe four years old, eating a floating sandwich in the bathtub, may or may not be true. But it still sums up everything that was brilliant and wonderful about my resourceful young mother in San Francisco in the 1960s. With sand-colored hair and full lips, she was slight and pretty and nervous like a bird, laughing and hopeful because hope was the only thing she could afford. She was about twenty-four at that time with a vivacious blond baby boy, a pondering dark-haired six-year-old boy, and me in between them, half-dark, half-light. My father thought she was a little crazy and sometimes told her this, in an angry and accusing voice. But she just smiled and looked away, pushing her thin hair in front of her eyes.

My mother loved babies. She loved, I imagine, how they needed her, how they—I mean we—reached out with our fingers and mouths, pulling on her nipples and her earrings and her hair, anchoring her to a living, breathing thing even more vulnerable than herself. Her father had been in the army and her mother had had the awful habit of denigrating her own daughters, so my mother grew up mobile yet unsure of her footing, glancing around always—like that bird—to make sure she was in the clear. She met my father not far from the army base in Monterey, California, when she was seventeen years old and living with a family that had taken her in when her mother kicked her out of the house. My father had come west from Brooklyn, New York, seeking poetry and jug wine and freedom and everything else that brought young curly-haired Jewish men from the East to California in 1959 or 1960. Instead he ran into my mother. They got pregnant, then married. Then they moved to San Francisco, where they got pregnant a second and a third time, one accident after another.

If you learn about California from books, you will read the word "abundance" over and over. Home to the world's largest fertile valley, this is the place where John Steinbeck's Okies thought they could grasp handfuls of ripe peaches just by reaching up. It's true: everything is warmer, easier, and more fruitful in California. But it is still possible, in the midst of all this wealth and beauty, to grow up deprived. People will ask me sometimes why my parents were poor. They were white, they were smart, they were attractive, they lived in America—in California, no less. Why weren't they successful? It is a question I do not understand. It is a question that makes me laugh and roll my eyes and then want to slap somebody. As if all you needed to make it in this country was the right stuff. As if to be rich were the better option, and they simply chose wrong or else were lazy or had a statement to make.

The simple answer is that neither of my parents was born into money, and neither of them ever learned to desire it much. They did not *decide* to be poor; they just were. And then, because money struck them as both unavailable and uninteresting, they didn't do much to change their circumstances. They were excited by art and literature and ideas and peace and justice, and they tried their hands at making these things instead of making money.

To complicate things further, my father suffered from a propensity to let others go first that bordered on martyrdom. The son of an immigrant garment salesman, he had gone to college just long enough to gather evidence for his theory that the only way a person became rich was by stepping on the backs of the poor and shoving their heads underwater. So he believed wealth was not only unattainable and undesirable, but also unethical. Yet it was circumstances more than philosophy that kept him in the working class. And then came the babies, too soon and too many, and making enough money became even harder.

While my father suffered from a slight case of self-righteousness, my mother suffered from a lack of confidence which made her see herself as unqualified to participate fully in life. With words and straps and other punishments, my grandmother, who was Polish and

Catholic from Queens, New York, had convinced her that she was not a whole person, and my mother never grew out of the feeling that she was not entitled to occupy space on the couch or dirty a plate or bother a salesclerk. She longed to go to college, but no one—not her mother; not the nuns who taught her in school; not her father, who stayed on at the Army base in Germany after the war—ever told her that she could.

My family on my mother's side was raised Catholic, but they placed their faith in luck. They prayed to luck, and wished and hoped for it as if it were the incarnation of Jesus himself. The baby brother, my grandmother's favorite, was revered for entering contests and winning cash, cars, cases of soda. Later, when my grandmother died and he figured out how to earn extra profit by selling her house without a real estate agent, it was celebrated in the family as if he had won the jackpot. My mother would describe this great feat with the unmistakable tic of awe in her voice, the same tic I would go on to hear all my life whenever she mentioned someone getting a bit of success in the form of a good job or husband, a published poem, a starring role in the play, as if achievement were a gift from the wily goddess of fortune.

Though luck was what my mother believed in—and banked on—she did not necessarily think it was ever going to fall to her. Many of those who play the lottery do so because they can see no other way out. In the years to come, her lottery would come in the form of poetry contests and academic scholarships, grants for community arts projects or writers-in-the-schools programs, though even if she won one of these from time to time it never seemed to propel her out of her poverty or hopelessness as she had imagined it would. But she would continue to believe in the big windfall and to mail in the self-addressed envelopes that just might bring it on. This attitude, of course, wore off on me, starting on that corner of 16th and Sanchez when us kids would shout, "That's my car" at any cool vehicle that drove by. As I got older, I would play the same game with apartments, houses, boyfriends, jobs, and vacations—hoping, wishing, praying, but not quite believing that any of it would ever come my way.

For my brothers and me, not having, and then wanting, started in earnest at the corner of 16th and Sanchez, when I was seven years old. The elementary school took up one side of that corner, and across the street the Arabs at the corner store sold beer, cigarettes, potato chips, popsicles, and flat, girlish bottles of liquor. The next corner had a bar, open all day and full of old men. And on the last corner stood an apartment house with a tall wooden fence painted dark brown. One time, from the front room of our third-floor flat, my brothers and I watched a guy walking naked in front of that wall. This was in 1970 in San Francisco, but still, it was unusual to see a man walk buck naked down the street as casual as could be. Us kids gawked and giggled until he went out of sight; then we called our friends who lived a block down so they, too, could look out their window and see him.

We had too much city in us to be real hippies, though

our parents sort of looked the part—our dad with his
little Jewish afro pulled into a tiny pigtail at the base of
his neck; our mom with her long hair and embroidered
blouses. Also, my dad smoked pot and made vases iout
of redwood and god's eyes out of wooden dowels, selling them on tables he set up on the street downtown and
in the tourist areas. But we knew who the real hippies
were. They were the kids with scraggly long hair, the ones
who didn't go to school because it was part of "the system". They were the kids next door, who lived in a big
old building with a storefront on the ground floor all
kinds of staircases and rooms and hallways filled with
various cats and people wandering around and curling
up on large pillows. We never knew who was related to
who, or what we would find when we opened a door. We
used to jump somehow from our back porch onto their
flat, tar-and-gravel roof, and then slide down air ducts
into rooms where people were sleeping or getting high or
making love.

We were friends with the hippie kids, but we weren't
hippies ourselves. We went to school and my brothers had
short hair, while mine tried so hard to stay brushed and in
barrettes or ponytails. Sometimes our clothes were ripped
or didn't match. But we didn't do it to be hippies. We did
it because we were poor and our mother was rushed, trying to take care of us and also work and go to class at the
city's junior college, and our father didn't notice things
like that. We liked the hippie kids, and we played with
them, though we mostly played in the schoolyard and
the alley with the other boys who had short haircuts and

moms who struggled to keep them tidy.

The school was massive—three stories tall and a whole city block long. I've been back as an adult, and it still looks as imposing as it ever did: stucco the color of terra cotta and a red tile roof, like an overgrown Spanish Colonial, with the blacktopped schoolyard, also a block long, hidden out back. The schoolyard for the junior high backed up against the yard for the elementary school, forming one huge, asphalt playground that was our universe. The boys played basketball and three-flies-up and threw pitches for each other against rectangular strike zones painted on the school walls while the girls played hopscotch and jump rope with rhymes and then went home to play jacks. My two brothers had two friends, also brothers, and I played with this foursome, except when they didn't let me. I stayed out with my brothers and the boys, waiting to get asked to join a side. The schoolyard was on a pretty good slant, and it was always better to have an extra person on hand to chase down a ball, so I often got in. Other times, there were enough boys and my brothers wouldn't argue my case, so I would slide my seven- or eight-year-old body under the iron prongs of the gate at the shortcut, and wander up the alley, looking in windows and doorways, kicking cans, listening to snatches of songs and arguments in Spanish and English, trying to figure out how this world around me worked.

The other kids in the neighborhood didn't have any more money than we did, but they did have more rules: no playing in your school clothes, no cussing, no staying out past dark. In my family, our school clothes were the same as our play clothes. We bought them on Mission Street, at the Value Giant, which later changed hands and became the Giant Value by just reversing the sign. Jeans, T-shirts, sneakers, maybe a little dress for me—my mother loved to put me in red—and blue-hooded sweatshirts with big pockets for warming our hands. We wore these clothes to play roller derby in the schoolyard, to eat hot lunch in the cafeteria, to go on field trips to the aquarium, where despite begging our mom for a can of soda in our bag lunch, we always found an orange instead—it was, she said, a better way to quench our thirst. We wore them to 24th Street where we bought Mexican pastries, and to Mission Street, home of cheap shoe stores and theatres that showed Cantinflas movies in Spanish or else had been converted into churches. We wore them to play with the family of four black kids who had no father and whose mother always had the belt at the ready, especially for the eldest, who was well-meaning but gregarious and prone to playing with us past dark or not keeping track of his younger brothers like he was supposed to. We wore them on Sundays, when the Mexican girls and boys dressed up in white and marched like miniature brides and grooms to the Mission Dolores for their First Holy Communion. We wore them to stand on our rickety back steps, perched high on the third floor overlooking the alleyway to the schoolyard, and to leap off those steps onto the flat roof of the hippie house next door.

I made that jump once and was playing with the hippie girl who was my age—she had one blue eye and one brown eye—when her mom asked her to get her dad from the bar on the corner diagonally across from us. We walked across one street and then another to the heavy swinging doors that faced the elementary school that I went to but she did not. The day was warm and bright. The bar was cave-dark inside and it stank of something humid and male: it was the smell of sweat and beer and cigarettes. The smell of piss and boasting and complaining. There was that sign about minors not allowed in, and I hesitated; even if I couldn't read it all the way, or was confused about why they wouldn't let in people who worked in mines, I knew this was not my place. But the hippie girl just walked straight into the darkness. She knew right where to find her dad; he had his seat at the end of the bar. I waited on the corner looking into the cave, then back out to the world I knew, the loud, fast corner of 16th and Sanchez, squinting against the sun and the sky and the cars zooming by. A few minutes passed, she emerged with her father, and we walked him home. At my house, we had a bottle of Japanese plum wine on a shelf in the kitchen, though I'd never seen my parents take more than a sip. My father smoked his pot and his cigarettes, but I never noticed anything other than the smell. I certainly couldn't imagine having to rescue him and get him home safely.

If you are a family that looks sort of like hippies, but hippies by accident—not like you decided to be poor but like you are trying as hard as you can to keep things together, to get gas money and milk money and rent money— sometimes people from the world of offices and suits and ties will look at you with disdain. But other times they will smile with compassion and pity at the three children in rumpled shirts squeezed into the cab of a big old pickup truck with a dad driving and a mom who looks too young to have all those kids.

One night in July, on my mother's birthday, we had left our corner and were driving around Fisherman's Wharf, a place we normally had no reason to visit, looking for something cheap but fancy to do. My mother was wearing her nice pants—not the jeans, but the light-brown ones with the grommets and the flare—and we were trying to find somewhere to bring her that would make her feel like she'd had a good reason for putting on those pants. When we saw the wax museum, the pictures of Dorothy and the Scarecrow, Frankenstein and the Werewolf, us kids yelled and pleaded. We were in the Woody, or maybe by then the Woody was gone and my father had bought the Ford sedan, removed the back seats, and replaced them with a plywood bench that could double as storage during camping trips. Or maybe we'd got rid of the Ford and were in my dad's white International, a truck with a bench seat long enough to fit all five of us.

My father stopped the truck; my mother got out to see how much it cost. Eventually I would learn that this is not necessarily the first question that everyone asks. But at the time, and for many years before and after, it was the only question that mattered. We sat in the truck, quiet, three sets of eyes watching my mother in a pantomime with someone hidden in a ticket booth. My father looked straight ahead, patient and pessimistic as always, not wanting to get too involved, even with—especially with—his own family, not wanting to be responsible for any possible disappointment. My mother leaned into the ticket window and smiled, then frowned. She gestured toward us in the truck, and we saw a head peer out and take a look in our direction then disappear back into the booth. Walking toward us, my mother had a bounce in her step that made her pant legs swing. "She'll let us all in for the price of one," she said. This was clearly a triumph, though my father still hesitated, wondering how much. But us kids were already spilling out of the truck onto the sidewalk and then filing past the lady in the ticket booth, a lady not much older than my mother, a lady who looked back at us with that smile of benevolence that I would come to know so well.

People gave us free stuff, and though we weren't quite sure why, we were too young to be ashamed by it. We took those quarters, the candy, the toys, the hand-me-down clothes that even strangers gave us. My mother may have cringed, but she couldn't quite say no. We were precocious little blonde-haired kids, inventing games with rocks or bottle caps or leftover fireworks or whatever else we found on the sidewalk; some people sneered, but many smiled and dug into their pockets and produced something for us and told us, when we balked, to take it and not tell our parents. Pretty soon we learned how to work it, and who it worked on, and who it did not work on. It worked on drunks, like the one who stumbled out of the bar, crossed the street diagonally to our Kool-Aid stand, and gave us five dollars for a sip of sugary purple water. People coming out of that bar were not in their right mind, I knew, and I tried to run after him to tell him he had given us too much. But my brothers grabbed me by the sleeve and held me back. "It's a *tip*," they said, using some new word they'd learned that was supposed to make it okay.

The cute-white-kid-in-ragged-clothes thing did not work on the Arabs at the corner store; we always had to pay full price, except on Halloween, when they'd give out regular-sized candy bars to the trick-or-treaters. And it especially did not work on Mr. Lee, the Chinese man at the other corner store down the block. His black eyes watched you from his low seat behind the counter where he kept all the candy, so you had to ask him for what you wanted, and he took your money before he handed you your stuff. The cute thing worked mostly on other white people, like the husband and wife on our block who had no kids and liked to invite us in for grilled-cheese sandwiches; like the gay couple who opened the stained-glass studio in the storefront after the gypsies moved out, and who let us play with their Irish setter puppies; like the lady at the wax museum.

In fourth grade I got bussed, along with the black and brown kids from the school around the corner, to a school in a white neighborhood. Every morning we boarded the yellow bus for a short ride up a hill and halfway down its other side, to a neighborhood with grass and trees and gardens and tennis courts in the park. I made friends with a girl there, white, who walked to school, a girl who would go on to become famous and rich. She decided we should pool our money so we could buy something big together. She instructed me to go through my house and collect all the loose change so we could add it to hers. I wasn't sure how to tell her that there was no unclaimed money at my house, not even pennies.

I wasn't sure how to tell her what I knew about money, because I could see that it was so very different from what she knew. This was a kind of knowledge that lived not in the head, but in the belly, the thighs, the throat, the shoulders. It affected one's gait and posture, the sound of one's voice. Next to this girl, I folded inward and loped behind. After school, when the bus returned me to my own neighborhood, I stood taller; I walked more solidly on the concrete that covered the earth; I yelled, open-throated and full of relief.

But daily, in school, I was beginning to learn shame. In my class picture, I am sitting in the front row, trying desperately to hide my feet under the bench. It's my shoes that I don't want recorded on film: black high-top Converse All-stars, my prized possessions, but the only shoes I have, and so I am wearing them with my picture-day dress.

On Halloween that year, I learned even more about money. Our neighborhood was on the outer edge of the Spanish-speaking Mission district, just where it started to nudge up against the Castro, just when that neighborhood was beginning to be inhabited by short-haired men wearing tight jeans, pink shirts, and, sometimes, black-leather chaps. The local hardware store had long sponsored a Halloween costume contest. They blocked off Castro Street and set up a platform where children, and grown men dressed as women, paraded across the stage in front of crowds and judges, until finally there was one person left standing there—and this year it was me, dressed as Raggedy Ann—receiving a red first-place ribbon and a gift certificate for ten dollars from the store.

By the time I was in high school, Halloween on Castro Street was a wild and raucous event, with suburban teenagers showing up to watch, and sometimes beat up, the drag queens and leather-chapped cowboys. By then, Harvey Milk had set up shop and gay men had arrived from Rochester and Cleveland and Minneapolis to stake this street as their own, sometimes looking at me as if I didn't belong here though I was the one that could actually call this street home. But as a child in the neighborhood, the Castro's Halloween street party was still a mix of kids, families, hippies, artists, and gays, all dressed in costumes that ranged from mild to inventive to outrageous. The year I won, my mother had sewn bloomers and a pinafore with frilly edges; my father had dyed a mop orange and turned it into a wig, then painted my face white, with sad black triangles under the eyes and cheerful red circles on the cheeks. Apparently the judges were sentimental, and they chose the rag doll over all the outrageousness.

A few days later the photos, taken by a professional photographer, were posted in the store window, each with their own number. The directions from my father were clear: walk up to the store and look at the pictures, write down the numbers of the photos with me in them, and then come back home so we could decide which ones to order. Probably it was the excitement of seeing myself in those glossy eight by tens, grinning with whiteface and glee. Probably it was the desire to preserve that glee, as if I knew somehow that it would end soon and I should have some evidence of this earlier me. But I took those numbers inside the store; I went up to the lady at the counter and started telling her that it was me in these pictures and she wrote down the numbers on a form and took down my name and phone number and just like that I had ordered the prints, all of them, eight by tens, which are quite large and expensive, an unnecessary extravagance when just a couple four by sixes of the truly important shots would suffice.

"Oh," said my father, when I got home. "You already ordered them." His voice was low, modulated, genuinely surprised, and not even accusatory. But his disappointment was almost mournful, and I wasn't sure which sin was greater: not following his instructions, or costing him money.

And then there was that ten-dollar gift certificate. This hardware and variety store was perhaps the world's greatest store, with everything you could possibly want including some things you didn't know you wanted, didn't even know existed, until you went in there and saw them on the shelf. It was the kind of store that I imagined Laura and her family got so excited about in those *Little House on the Prairie* books, when a trip into town to shop was the biggest event of the season. My dad would stop in for screws and bolts, to get a key made, and maybe pickup a quarter-pound of chocolate-covered jelly sticks at the candy counter. Us kids would spend our pennies, nickels, and dimes on super balls and jacks, army figurines, jump ropes, yo-yos, and other treasures made out of plastic and metal. Cliff's sold stationery, dishes, toasters, brooms, and safety pins. They sold crayons, paint, glitter, and glue; bolts of fabric and rolls of ribbon and lace. They sold model airplane kits and basketballs and roller skates. In other words, they sold all kinds of stuff that a nine-year-old girl might love to buy with a ten-dollar gift certificate.

But I didn't know how to take ten dollars and spend it on myself. I had no practice in doing such a thing, not even as a witness. I knew only how to scrimp and salivate, how to yearn for things that I understood I would never actually have. This particular shade of yearning—yellow-green, almost chartreuse—would go on to comfort and frustrate me for much of my life. It was waiting for me when I was born, and the thin, constant nausea it gave off was as familiar to me as the locks of hair on my neck that I used to twirl around my fingers. It filled my every cell with the certainty that there's always more out there, and something to feel empty about. And eventually that glum certainty became the one thing I could count on in a life full of promise and impossibility.

Leonard Cohen has a song in which a voice says from a doorway, "You must not ask for so much," while another cries out, "Hey, why not ask for more." Even at that age, young enough to dress up as sad-and-happy Raggedy Ann, I was caught between those two doorways. When

Porsches and Jaguars drove down 16th Street every once in a while like visitors from another planet, I would lust after them, claiming them in a shrill and confident voice. But underneath that voice, wrapped in a pale, putrid green, was the realization that I'd never get one, that, in fact, I wouldn't know what to do with one if I did. My imagination was large, but when it came time to manifest itself, it shriveled up like wool socks in the dryer. I simply could not visualize anything coming true.

So I squandered that gift certificate on inexpensive trinkets for my family and myself—a noble idea, but driven more by guilt than desire. Christmas was coming up, and I took that official, signed paper into the store three or four or five times, picking out an egg timer for my father (who liked his boiled at just three minutes), some new Hot Wheels for my brothers, and barrettes for my mother and me. It shows good character to think of others ahead of oneself, but my parents had perhaps taught me too well; a nine-year-old girl should have an instinct for buying herself a toy. Each time I visited the store, large expensive things leered at me from the top shelf, where children and thieves could not get to them; but I ignored the roller skates, the remote-controlled car, the backyard water slide I'd seen advertised on television with ecstatic, wet children, and instead I had the clerk subtract $3.50 or $2.75 until finally I had piddled away my ten dollars on a bunch of small, useless stuff that would soon be broken or lost.

CHAPTER 2
GET INTO CARS WITH STRANGERS

There comes a time in every girl's life when she meets a man who leers. My first leer—or the first one I recognized—came at the comic book store on 22nd Street, just down from the fruit market on Mission with its bins of cascading lemons, peppers, and papayas. When I was seven years old, my father, who collected Marvels and DCs, took us kids there one day, and while he and my older brother checked out Spiderman and Silver Surfer, my younger brother and I headed for Richie Rich, Casper, and Archie. When it was time to leave, we made our selections, put the rest back on the rack, and watched the man at the counter stack them up and slip them into a flat brown paper bag just made, it seemed, for holding comic books. We took the bag—I don't know who got to carry it—and stepped outside back into the raucous sounds and colors that are Mission Street on a Saturday afternoon. The shop owner, potbellied and bearded, in a tie-dyed T-shirt like Jerry Garcia, followed us out, to get a touch of sun maybe, and another eyeful of me.

"I know just what she's going to look like when she

gets older," he said to my father, and the way he said it made him sound as if he also knew what I was going to *be* like, as if I were no longer a seven-year-old girl, but was now a future woman, a potential bed partner, a heart-breaker-in-training.

My father knew this man slightly through their mutual interest in comic books, but he didn't know how to take a remark like this, and so he ignored it. Though I looked away, searching for something—a shoelace, a hub-cap—to set my eyes upon, I could not ignore it. This was the first time I'd been separated out from my brothers by sex, not just gender, and all I wanted was to disappear, to shrink behind my father's legs and meld back into the comfortable unit my brothers and I had always been— three kids alternately playing, teasing, and fighting—and that we'd been a half-hour earlier when we came into the shop. Not only the man, but now my father and my broth-ers, too, were looking at me differently. A rotting smell wafted over from the fruit bins on the corner. Cars drove by spitting out exhaust. My stomach turned. Finally, we took our bag of comics and left.

Shortly after this incident, I got moved into my own room—something of a feat, as there were three competi-tive kids at our house and two rooms between us. First we'd all slept in "the kids' room," and used the second one as a playroom. Then we were separated by age, with the oldest getting his own room, and the two younger ones sharing. But one day my father painted the smaller of the two rooms powder blue and then, when it dried, he cut a roll of royal-blue contact paper into a silhouette of a castle, with turrets and moats and drawbridges and quarter moon slices hanging in the sky, pasting it around the four walls at my eye level. Perhaps this was the best way he knew to take care of me: not to defend or shield or explain, but to create a paper fortress in the little room at the end of the hallway for me to slip into. And though the coveted room was lovely and I was proud to have it, sometimes, at night, in bed, down the hall from everyone else, I felt more banished than pampered.

Also about this time, us kids—my brothers and I and their two best friends from down the block—discovered pornography. We found it in a wooden box at the top of a cedar tree outside of the junior high on Church Street. We were roving the neighborhood like a pack of wild puppies, looking for something (an empty lot, or say a hole in a fence) to get into, when we noticed a large wooden box sitting on the top branches like an oversized bird's nest. Quick and agile, I was the one who scurried up that tree fastest and highest, got my hands onto the box, and pushed it down so it busted open in the dirt with a loud smack, spilling out *Playboy* magazines at the feet of the boys below.

Now *that* was a treasure chest we did not expect. What were we to do with those magazines and how did they get there in the first place? The box was too big and heavy to carry up the tree, so it had to have been thrown out one of the windows from the second floor of the school right above it. Maybe it was a teacher, or a janitor, or a dirty old man—we'd heard about these kinds of men, though we didn't know what exactly they did that dirtied them.

But more urgent than finding out where these magazines came from was figuring out where they would go. We knew they were something we weren't supposed to see, and we had to get them hidden before anyone getting off the streetcar walked by and found us with them. So we packed them back into the rickety wooden box, dragged it into the bushes, and divvied them up between us. Opening those pages, we found shiny women squinting back at us, lips parted, underwear undone, and I giggled along with the boys. But as I looked at these women who seemed almost swollen, their body parts so large and so round, I had to wonder if this was what that man at the comic store had meant, if this was what I was going to look like when I grew up.

Pornography, I found out soon afterwards, could also be delivered to your house. I was just discovering the magic of the mail, in which you got a stamp, licked it, and stuck it on an envelope with a series of words and numbers placed on certain lines and in certain corners; then you put it in the big blue metal box on the street corner, and somehow that envelope arrived somewhere else, maybe even across the country or around the world. I didn't know how it worked exactly—there were people who picked it up, and people who delivered it, and lots of people in between—but I was amazed at the invisible network that resulted in these envelopes getting slipped through the slot on our front door every day at about the same time, landing in a small pile on the floor. One day I happened to be the one who came home first, unlock-ing the door with my key, which I wore on a cord around my neck. My brothers must have been out playing, and my parents out working or running errands, so I picked up the little pile, as if they were party favors, and carried them up the sixty-four stairs (Or was it fifty-six, or maybe forty-eight stairs? I know I counted them every single time I went up or down, as if to reassure myself, but now that number, once so solid and dependable, is gone from my mind.) And as I climbed, I examined the stamps, the postmarks, the writing saying who the letters were to and who they were from. One piece, thick like a magazine but wrapped in brown paper, was addressed to someone who'd lived at our house before we did, and occasionally still got mail delivered here. And inside the paper wrapper—I just had to open it—there was a little booklet whose pages were covered with photographs the size and shape of postage stamps, but instead of birds and presidents, the pictures showed naked men and women, mostly women, doing all sorts of things to each other that I had never seen or even imagined. Words underneath the pictures told what the naked people were doing, and how you could see more if you sent in money for movies that could be sent to you also through the mail. The colorful *Playboy* photos had seemed almost wholesome compared to these, which made my stomach queasy and filled my mind with images that would not fall out of my head no matter how hard I shook it. I knew it was wrong to open someone else's mail, but I hadn't known *how* wrong.

And then there is more than leering. There is showing and touching, the opening of zippers and buttons, the quivering of the upper lip, the beading of sweat on the forehead. There is the girl I was, eight years old now, jumping rope outside her home, around the corner from the elementary school. There is the boy from the neighborhood walking by, stopping to see if my big brother is home. And there is the man without a face, without a body, but with a car—white, maybe, big, American—who pulls up to the curb to ask for directions to the Golden Gate Bridge, which is nowhere near where we live, and since we're only kids, we don't know how to get anyplace, anyway, except to the schoolyard and the corner store. And then the car is driving away and the boy is continuing on down the street looking for my brother or some other boys to play with, and I am back to jumping rope in front of my house, alone but surrounded by people waiting at the crosswalk, going in and out of the corner store across the street, driving down busy 16th Street and across Sanchez. And then there is the big white car again, with the faceless man pulling up to the curb.

This time he is looking not for the bridge, but for his son, who he describes to me but who I haven't seen, though I suggest he try the schoolyard. And because the faceless man needs help finding his little boy, we figure out that I can go in one entrance to the schoolyard, and he can go in the other, at the other end of the long block, and we can meet in the middle. In this way we will be covering all the ground between us and making sure we look everywhere. And so I run down the alleyway to the schoolyard, which is as large as a city block, but open and empty, unusually empty—where are my brothers and their friends, where are the girls playing hopscotch, the kids shooting baskets or trying out a new bike? Instead, I find the man but not his boy. And somehow the man, who has no voice either, suggests that I get into his car to help him search the neighborhood, and soon I am in the passenger seat and the sights outside the window are getting less and less familiar. And now the man who has no face is smiling at me; the man who has no voice is talking to me, telling me what a pretty and nice girl I am; the man who has no body is unzipping his pants and holding his thing in his hands and breathing in a loud rasp and trying to talk me into sucking his dick, which, he says, tastes like a lollipop.

It is at this point that the world cracks open, revealing something slippery at its core. At this moment, with this man holding his thing with one hand and the steering wheel with the other, and me squeezing myself as far away as possible, trying to melt into the door. From now on, the world is always a little gray no matter how sunny, and any look, any talk, is suspect. From now on, all men are faceless, all cars are dangerous, and anytime anyone appreciates my beauty they are trying to get something from me that I won't give up. Sex, danger, and lollipops. My stomach is turning, my eyes are squeezing shut, and I am saying, either in my head or out loud, "Please let me out, please let me out," and trying to figure out where we are, and if the door is locked, and what exactly happens to a person who jumps out of a moving car.

Finally, somehow, the car is back in front of the school-yard, heading toward the curb, the heavy metal door is swinging open, and my feet are reaching for the sidewalk, then running around the corner to my landing and up the sixty-four (or fifty-six or forty-eight) steps into the front room where my parents are sitting in the quiet afternoon sun with papers and pens and checkbooks as if nothing at all has happened. The good news is that the man did not follow through on his threats. He placed his hand on my head, nudged it toward his lap, but did not force it all the way there. So I jumped out of that car scared, nauseous, irrevocably aged, but relatively untouched—in fact my skin was hardening at that very moment into a shell that would protect me from leers and even benign touching for many years to come. The good news is that my parents both happen to be home, and they wrap me in their arms and want to hear the whole story.

The bad news is that they are young parents who married and had children by some combination of accident and optimism. The bad news is that my brothers happen to be out, and my father happens to think, in the wisdom of his inexperience, that the best thing would be to keep it among the three of us, and not tell anyone else what's happened—not my teacher, not the kids at school, not even my brothers, even if up until this moment they know every single thing about me. My parents believe— or at least they hope—that it will all be forgotten if we just don't talk about it. Perhaps they feel guilty at forgetting to tell their children not to get into cars with strangers, at being unable to protect their daughter when she was just downstairs while they were sitting with coffee cups and cigarettes and paperwork. They try their best, but they are overwhelmed with juggling bills and paychecks, offspring and aspirations, truth and beauty. They don't realize that silence, like the turrets of a paper castle around a blue bedroom wall, will only serve to make me feel more confused, ashamed, and alone.

The bad news is that this was only my introduction to all the things that men will do to girls, that there would be more incidents as I wandered my neighborhoods in this city and the world beyond. The bad news is that a hard shell is indiscriminate; it keeps the flowers out as well as the weeds, and a girl can grow up to become a woman without ever shedding that calcareous skin. The bad news is that, though I will eventually blank out his face, I cannot forget this man, nor the tenuous, earthquake-y feeling I get every time I remember what he did to me. While it's true that he barely put a hand on me, he left his mark in other, more indelible ways.

I was seven, eight, and nine when we lived on the corner of 16th and Sanchez, though it feels like I spent my whole childhood there. Many pieces of information about the world came to me in those few years—news, sometimes conflicting, about sex and money and violence, about girls and boys and the women and men they became. Some of that information came from arguments, from people on the street or even my parents in the front room, after we'd gone to bed. The next morning we'd find a broken chair or a pair of scissors with one blade cracked off, and wonder if arguing had transformed our normally reasonable dad into something like the Hulk. From the evening news, we'd learned about a serial killer named the Zodiac who was on the loose in our city, leaving a trail of cryptic clues. He was as tall as the drainpipe on the school building, they said at recess, and was supposed to do things that sounded so unfathomable I wasn't sure if he was real or from one of those comic books my dad liked to read. From magazines and movies and television and even just people walking down the street, I learned how boys were supposed to look at girls and how girls were supposed to return those looks. It was a slanted, knowing look from the man, sneaking a peek in plain view, like the looks on the faces of the men on the Black Velvet Whiskey billboards mounted so low onto the sides of buildings that we almost could have reached up and put our hands on the cleavage spilling out of the lady's dress.

Not everything we learned was upsetting, and our house was filled with laughter as well as yelling. Even with the street traffic, we could hear my father's hearty cackle from three stories down, as we played on the sidewalk and he sat at his drafting table in the front room, listening to the game on the radio, reaching into his coffee cans full of pencils, sharpening them with a silver Exacto knife to give them blunt, naked tips, then sketching out the plans for his next art piece or some furniture we needed for the house. He may have been stoned, taking hits off his palm-sized wooden pipe, but even when he wasn't, that laugh erupted and flowed. My mother's laugh was brighter, not quite as loud, as she found something absurd about the world to delight in: the way the cat licked his mustache, as if embarrassed about his messiness; the way I promised,

in a Mother's Day card, to clean the empty cans off the
back porch as my present to her. Since I found those same
things to be funny, I often joined her with my junior version of her own laugh. My light brother had an infectious
giggle, while my dark brother usually tried to contain his
laughter with a sly smile, almost devious, as he came up
with a plan—to rig up buzzers for his version of a TV quiz
show, or to map all the pay phones in a three-block radius
and station someone at each phone at a specified time to
receive a call from him back home at headquarters.

There was music in our house, too: my mother singing, and alternately gliding and stalling as she learned to
play guitar, strumming out folk songs like Oh My Darling, Clementine and Woody Guthrie's Union Maid ("Oh,
you can't scare me, I'm sticking to the union"), sometimes even trying a Beatles song from her green-and-
white songbook. On the record player came Joan Baez
and Pete Seeger with more rousing protest songs, Johnny
Cash from Folsom Prison, and Bob Dylan, a thin man
with loose dark curls who looked sort of like my father.
And while the music was playing, we created things from
scratch. We folded little stacks of paper in half, stapled
them down the spine, and drew panels of large squares
across and down each page. Then we filled each square
with our own superheroes—such as Captain Cobra, who
had the speed and sneakiness of a snake—adding cap-
tions below and bubbles of dialogue above. Seeing our
handmade comic books, my father invented a wooden
machine that allowed us to animate our own moving
pictures. He mounted a roll of butcher paper on a dowel

on one side of a plywood screen, then put another dowel on the other side, as a take-up reel. We would draw our scenes, then stand behind the movie box and narrate as we cranked the handles attached to the dowels, moving the paper "film" from reel to reel.

Once, a few days after Christmas, my brothers, the two brothers from down the block, and I created our own holiday. The evening sky was already dark as we roved the neighborhood collecting all the trees that had been tossed out on the sidewalk, awaiting the garbage truck. Then we dragged those discarded trees to the alley by the schoolyard, and set them up in a circle, our own ever-green forest. We'd just had Christmas, had torn colored paper off ridiculous amounts of presents, even if many of those packages were filled with soap or socks. But we wanted more. So we went off in search of gifts—penny candy from the corner store; a Hot Wheels we no longer wanted—and wrapped them up in the remnants of colored paper plucked from the trash, then reconvened in our alley forest to give and receive all over again.

One of the great joys of childhood at that time and place was just walking out the door, saying "I'm going out to play," over your shoulder. Not even the man in the car could take that pleasure away from me. I'd scoot around the corner to the schoolyard with my bike or a skateboard I'd snatched from a brother, and see who else was around. Maybe I'd practice making that sharp turn at the end of the long alley without falling off the skateboard. Maybe I'd join in a round of jump rope with the girls or basketball with the boys, practicing my waterbug-style defense, sticking on my man, then, when he turned around for the shot, flailing my short arms and legs every which way, in my only hope to deter him. Maybe I'd walk up to the baseball diamond painted on the blacktop just as a handful of kids were trying to get enough players together for three-flies-up. I'd borrow a mitt, take my place in the field, and train my eyes on the ball as it got pitched, pitched again, then smacked. From the ball to my chest was an invisible string, so when the ball flew off the bat, my body moved back, then forward, then over a few steps. Finally I'd open my glove and stick out my hand so the ball could land right into it as if it had been aiming there all along. "One down," I'd yell, as free and happy as a child could be.

Eventually, however, I stumbled upon infinity, perhaps the most harrowing discovery of all, even more frightening than sex. I found it in the bathroom of our flat. We had two bathrooms, one with a sink and a tub, and the other, a small box of a room called a water closet, just big enough for a toilet. I used to go into that little room and close my eyes so it was dark, like the universe. Away from noise and light, from my brothers and the kids in the schoolyard, from the traffic on the street and the people buying cans of beer in paper bags at the corner store, I felt alone and inconsequential and wondered what it would be like if I were gone altogether or if I had never even been. Concentrating very hard, I could make myself disappear. Then I moved on to my brothers, and imagined them not being, either. Not the younger one with his light hair and laughing eyes; not the older one with

his dark hair and observing eyes. Like a lit fuse, I worked
my way through my family to the house, the block we
lived on, the whole city, the country. Eyes squeezed tight,
I pictured the planet, blue and green against black. "What
if there was no earth?" I asked myself, and poof, it disappeared, leaving the wide open space of the universe—a
dark hole with no shape that went on forever.

I stayed in infinity as long as I could stand it. Then I
threw open the door of that little room and ran down the
hall, looking for something to touch or see or hear. Just
the sound of my father sharpening a pencil in the front
room or my mother running the water in the kitchen
helped get me back to earth.

But once you know a thing like this you can never
un-know it, and from then on I was dodging infinity, trying to escape from the knowledge of how fragile and arbi-
trary everything is, how I and everything in this world,
indeed the world itself, could just as easily not exist. The
best way to avoid infinity was to stay occupied—with
games, chores, family fights—so there was no room for
wondering. But I couldn't stop myself; I was curious. It
was wonder that had led me to infinity in the first place,
and I went on that voyage again and again, the way people
go back on heroin or roller coasters. I did not yet know
that infinity was another word for despair, something
that would be coming soon enough. I did not yet realize
how so many things you never even thought about could
just get taken away from you.

CHAPTER 3
BEWARE THOSE FITS OF OPTIMISM

The eviction notice arrives in the mail, just like any other
bill or letter. There's no sheriff, no knock at the door, no sign
posted for everyone in the neighborhood to see. The mail-
man just slips the envelope through the slot on our door at
the corner of 16th and Sanchez, and it sits in that little pile
of mail on the floor until I come home from school, opening the door with the key that I wear around my neck and
calling upstairs to find no one home, then scooting up that
long staircase to our apartment two steps at a time. I put
the envelope on the kitchen table, next to a jar of pencils
and pens. Later that night when my parents have a spare
moment, one of them will open the letter and read it and
then read it again. It doesn't matter that they've got three
kids and a broken-down car and Dad is sort of working
and sort of trying to be an artist; it doesn't matter that it's
the middle of the school year and they've always paid the
rent on time and kept the place relatively quiet and clean.
It's just that the building has been sold and the new owners,
a young couple so excited to be moving to San Francisco,
want to live in the third-floor flat we happen to call home.

We visit courtrooms, stalling. My father does not have a suit or tie, so he puts on his least paint-stained shirt and pants and takes one or two of us kids downtown to plead his case. But it's no use. Soon enough we are packing up boxes and loading them into the blue Ford pickup with the homemade wooden camper on the back. It's a sunny, cool day in June. School just got let out for summer, and the neighborhood is saturated with children and noise.

Upstairs, my mother is piling our belongings into boxes, which we kids will then carry down the stairs so Dad can load them onto the truck the right way, the way that doesn't waste space or break anything. We have moved several times now, but we are not necessarily getting any better at it. Mom is running behind with the packing, so Dad has to wait on the street with the truck double-parked. My brothers, who have turned six and eleven, and I, nine, sit on the stoop, listening to the chorus of kid sounds emanating from the schoolyard: the *thwack* of the bat hitting a ball; the *thump* of the basketball against the backboard; the angry trill of voices arguing over fair or foul.

My father sighs, glances at the traffic he's disrupting, then looks over at us. "Why don't you go help your mother?" he says. It's not exactly a command, but neither is it a question. I run up the staircase, counting the steps for one of the last times. The carpeting on the steps is deep red, but faded. The wall is creamy white with a band of molding at my eye level that follows the curve of the stairs all the way to the hallway of our flat. In the kitchen I find my mother, frantic with newspaper and tape and marking pen, emptying shelves of dishes into cardboard boxes.

"Is he ready for another one?" she asks, her face framed by thin bangs and feather earrings.

"Uh, yeah," I say, trying to sound casual. When Dad gets mad, Mom gets flustered. She moves faster, but she accomplishes less. To preserve some sort of peace, I've got to get boxes packed and down the stairs. "Just shove that stuff in there, Mom," I say, piling plates into a box.

"But some is coming with us and some is staying," she explains. These boxes and our furniture—the kitchen table, the toy chest my father made, a few beds and chairs—will go to a friend's garage. Then we will load the rest, plus some camping gear, into the homemade camper, and face the truck brazenly to the north, toward optimism. The plan is to cross over the Golden Gate Bridge and look for Land—my father pronounces this word as if it were a proper noun—so we can get out of the city, escape the corner of 16th and Sanchez, and live a better life in the country. The country is a place we know something about because we've gone camping there. I have even spent time there on my own, at a summer camp in the Sierra Nevada foothills, a camp that grants scholarships to city kids below a certain income level so that we, too, may learn horseback riding, water skiing, archery, and how to twist colored plastic threads into a keychain.

We kids don't know much about my father's plan; we're not supposed to ask too many questions. If we do, he will sigh, take a drag off his cigarette, and look away, disappointed again. It's not clear how much of the plan even my mother knows, though surely they have discussed it, probably late at night after we have gone to bed. Perhaps it was these discussions that caused some of those muffled bangs and raised voices that seeped through the walls and into our bedrooms, infiltrating our dreams. We'd wake up in the morning to find a broken ashtray, the kid-sized table turned upside down, chairs strewn around the living room as if left there by the tide.

My mother and I fill three boxes, and I carry one downstairs and hand it to my dad, who's leaning on the back of the tailgate, smoking. My brothers have taken this opportunity to run off and play, and my father has chosen to ignore their disappearance. So I yell out for them, raising my voice above the sounds of balls and bats, cars and children, and they come running back. Eventually, we get all of our belongings loaded into the truck.

The next day, after the boxes and furniture have been delivered to the friend's house, we kids are loaded into the back of the truck ourselves. The truck starts up, and we look out the camper windows at our city slipping out from underneath us. The Plexiglas distorts the houses and streets and mutes the colors and sounds, so it is like watching a movie of our own life. My father has outfitted the camper as if it were a child's fort on wheels, with pillows and foam and sleeping bags. He's even installed an intercom, so we can buzz him and Mom in the cab to let them know who's hogging blankets or not sharing the snacks. But before we have even crossed that great orange bridge and the thick choppy water of the bay, my father has disconnected the intercom. When we bang on the cab

window, our parents turn around, shrugging, and pointing to the microphone on their end, as if to say, "It broke."

Our first stop is a cold, foggy beach. My brothers and
I are released from the truck like air from a tire, and we
scatter off to find driftwood for a campfire. We help pitch
our five-man tent behind dunes and out of the wind.
Then we tighten up the hoods on our blue sweatshirts
and go to play tag with the thick, foamy surf. Signs warn
of rip tides, undertows, and sneaker waves, but we don't
need signs to tell us that that we are not supposed to enter
this water. Its danger advertises itself: thick gray wedges
curl into sharp peaks before smacking with a loud *pop*
against the sloping beach. A chaos of churning white
foam rustles through the pebbly sand and sneaks, indeed,
high onto the beach. We run up, up, and away, to the dry
sand, where the thunder of the surf subsides, and we give
in to gravity and geography and emotion, dropping onto
that dark, pigeon-colored sand, our faces to the sky. Back
at the campsite, our parents are starting the stove and
unloading food from the ice chest. We have no place to
live, and no one, not even my father, knows where we are
going next. But we have maps and sleeping bags and piles
of comic books. We have flecked metal dishes—a different color for each of us—and a bulky can of kerosene.
We have yelling and kicking and whispering. We have an
intercom that sometimes mysteriously stops working.
And we have this plan of my father's to find Land.

And so we smile, my brothers and I, not at each other,
but at the benevolent gray sky above us. And we begin to
swing our arms and legs in slow, deliberate arcs through

the sand, etching out the West Coast version of snow angels. And then we try to get up without smudging our wings.

The next morning we head inland, where it is warm and golden just like the summer we have read about in books and seen on TV, and we begin the long search for a place to live. We sit in the wide, fancy car of a real-estate agent—my dad up front, three kids and my mom in back, the man in the suit glancing in his rearview mirror as we pinch each other and push the buttons to make the windows go up and down, up and down. We spend a day, but not the night, at a commune with real hippies who swim naked in the creek out behind the house while we city kids keep our bathing suits firmly on. We look for maps and pay phones and For Sale signs and little colored markers that show the edges of a piece of property. We park the car on the side of the road and trudge into the blackberry bushes and poison oak, into the mass of trees and brush that would have to be taken down somehow to make room for a house.

We stay as long as they'll let us at a campground on a warm, shallow lake where my father teaches us to fish and my mother teaches us to swim and—even better—to float. Standing in the lake up to her belly, she has me lie back in her arms, as if I were still a baby.

"Relax," she says. "Breathe." Her voice, not quite a whisper, is soothing and authoritative at the same time. My body complies: it softens and stretches out as if laying itself on top of a mattress. Inch by inch she slips her arms out from under me, going from hands to palms to fingertips, and finally letting go, but hovering close by in case I panic. My brothers are playing nearby, but the world seems hushed, like that time we went to church at the cavernous Spanish mission on 16th Street.

"Good," she says. "Keep breathing."

The water comforts and cradles me. My mother, still within reach, smiles. And I also smile, at the miracle of floating face up to the clouds while the thin green water somehow keeps my body aloft. This, too, is a kind of infinity, where the lines between me and the trees and the water and my mother's hands almost disappear, but it feels just fine.

The following morning my brothers and I wake up early, as usual, unzip the tent flap, then zip it back behind us, leaving our parents sleeping. We put on sweatshirts and navy blue knit caps, get out our enamel mugs and bowls, and make cereal and cold hot chocolate. Then we carry those mugs, which we pretend are beer steins, to the picnic table of the empty campsite down the gully from ours. The beer steins make us think of gangsters, and so we start calling each other "Mugsy" and "Bugsy" and "Moe." To feel more like criminals, we pull the knit caps down low on our foreheads, until we can barely see out from under them.

"What's the plan, Mugsy?" my older brother asks me.

"I don't got the plan, Moe. I thought you had it."

"I do have it," he says, reaching down to the ground and picking up an old metal fork from the dirt. "I was just testing you." He uses the fork to etch a few map-like lines onto the picnic table. Bugsy and I lean in close for the details.

When we finish up our cocoa, we raise our mugs and slam them down on the table. Then we get up to rove around the campground, looking for any loot previous campers may have left behind. The sun is up, though not enough to warm us, and the campground is beginning to come to life. Crows and Steller's Jays squawk at each other, and thin curls of smoke rise up from resuscitated campfires. After we've canvassed an empty campsite for several quiet, serious minutes, my little brother's voice beckons from the fire pit.

"Look," he says in a stage whisper, and he holds out his treasure: one of those aluminum pie pans stuffed with popcorn that we have seen on television. The popcorn bursts through the lid like confetti when you heat it. We know from the commercials that you can cook the popcorn by holding it over a campfire, but we have never dreamed that we would actually put our hands on this thing and all the adventure it promised. Now the littlest, the blondest, the luckiest of us three is holding in his outstretched hands a completely unpopped pan wrapped in shiny foil, the tantalizing blue-and-white cardboard label intact.

"Whoa," we older two say, instinctively reaching for the silver package. It is all we can do to wait till nightfall so we can scavenge wood and start a fire and cook our popcorn just like we imagine all the other families did on camping trips.

—

After miles of freeways and highways and dusty country roads, we finally land in a little trailer my father borrows from a friend, just a few miles from a brown body of water called, for some reason, Clear Lake. With no water or electricity, my parents camp in the trailer, and we pitch the tent alongside as a kind of kids' room, to give them some privacy. We cook and wash outside, with a Coleman stove and buckets of water, and we drive to the lake to swim and cool off and use the public restroom. Every once in a while—like when the whole family gets poison oak—we go to the other side of the lake, where they have a beach and a campground and a shower, and we carry our soap and towels into the concrete stalls to scrub ourselves clean.

Other than the corner of 16th and Sanchez in San Francisco, Clear Lake is the best place a kid could live. We spend all day in shorts and bathing suits, wandering back and forth between water and land. We turn over boulders, logs, and old tires to look for salamanders and potato bugs. We collect apricot pits and use them like coins, to buy stuff off each other. We rearrange the rocks on the beach, to create forts and moats and channels and deltas.

Standing in the murky water, we dig our toes into the soft mud bottom, feeling for clams, then dive under and grab them, tucking them into our bathing suits until we can get them to the bucket on shore. Then we smash them open on the rocks, stick a hook through the squishy lump inside, and drop the hook over the side of the dock. You don't even need a fishing pole, just a couple feet of kite string with a hook tied on the end, and if you don't have a hook you can use a safety pin. Eager, flat fish the size of our hands or a little bigger hop onto the line: blue-gill, sunfish, croppie. As long as we are quiet, they come round. We try every bait we can think of: night crawlers and lures and gooey red fish eggs out of a jar and balls of rolled-up Wonder Bread like our dad used to do when he was a kid. Those happy little fish are so crazy and bored they will jump onto an empty hook just to have some-thing to do. So we pull them up and grab them firmly, like our dad had showed us: just behind the head where the sharp back fins can't prick us. We hold onto their slipperi-ness as we back the hook out of their lip. Then we look for a good long while at their iridescent pond-colored skin and clear, wet scales glistening in the sun; at their round, startled eyes; at our hands gripping something beautiful and wild and helpless. And then we toss them back into the water with a splash.

Summer went on and on, for three, four, five months. My parents read the want ads, then dropped us kids off at the lake with cheese sandwiches while they drove around looking for work and for that little piece of Land upon which my father was going to build us a house—or at least a lot with water and septic so we could hook up the trailer and make it through winter. At the lake, my broth-ers and I learned how to ration the food to make it last all day, and how to make friends with the families who had coolers and inner tubes and bright plastic buckets with matching shovels, so perfect for carrying clams. We learned to do the backstroke and the deadman's float, to talk underwater, to flip the canoe over and then back, to repair the rafts with duct tape or chewing gum until Dad could do it the right way, with glue and a rubber patch. I outgrew my one-piece bathing suit, sky blue with white clouds, so my mother cut it into a two-piece, sewing a drawstring into the top and bottom seams. We gathered walnuts off the ground—they had to be roasted to taste any good—and we ate apricots and cherries from farm stands and sometimes even ice cream at Foster's Freeze, where the bug zapper flashed loud blue lightning all night long.

What struck us most about the country was how quiet it was—also how hot and still. Playing in the hills around the trailer, we hushed up instinctively; our voices, even when we were not shouting, stood out. We missed the noise of 16th and Sanchez, and the kids in the neighborhood, the way you could just walk out your door and find someone to play with. But we trusted our dad to know what was best for us, and we found plenty to do in the country. Outside, it was like one giant empty lot to explore and climb and chase and find things in. Inside our tent, we'd read comic books or play board games, or set up a miniature trade show, trying to talk each other into buying or trading all the little treasures (rocks, coins, toys, bottles) we'd found. There was infinity in the dry brown soil, in the crackly straw-colored grass, just as there was in the schoolyard and on the street corner. But the thing about infinity, about yearning and uneasiness and the heat of the breezes off the lake and the hills, is that as long as you can say "we," everything is somehow all right. My parents would argue and worry, and every once in a while they'd call a serious family meeting to discuss our shrinking options, but for the kids, camping in the country was either fun or boring, rarely tragic.

One late afternoon my father told us to go out and play and not to come back to the trailer till we were called. We ran off, but we forgot something—a flashlight? a pocket knife?—and I was elected to go back and retrieve it.

Standing at the trailer door, I heard noises, and wondered if my mother was all right. Hesitant to knock, I looked up at the yellow hills and the crooked oaks silhouetted against the bleached blue sky. The Indians used to gather the acorns from those trees and pound them into a meal, then cook up a kind of porridge with it. But first they had to shell the acorns, then soak and rinse the soft flesh over and over, to get rid of the bitterness that could make you sick. It took a long, long time and lots of water to make those acorns palatable, to turn them from poison into food.

From inside the trailer came the sounds of bodies in negotiation. I knew these noises; I had heard them in that car—white, maybe, big, American—on Sanchez Street. They'd frightened me then, and now I hated them all over again. Was this what sex was, a man trapping a woman in a small space, and making her do things to his body? It sounded sour and dangerous, like two cats about to claw each other. So I banged my arm on the door, partly to get the flashlight or knife I had come for, but mostly to break up whatever was going on in there.

"Go away," said the voice of my father.

And I did. I ran back to my brothers, and together we climbed into the hills, toward the low, gnarled oaks, who reached out their mossy branches and scooped us up.

Who knows where my father got his dream of bringing up his kids in the country; who knows where that sudden burst of optimism and intention came from, or where it would soon disappear to? He was a city kid from Brooklyn, though he'd gone fishing occasionally as a child, in the lakes and ponds upstate. But his preference for the country was grounded more in ideology than in experience. He felt instinctively that the city, like money, was evil and impure, and that in the country people could live the way humans were supposed to live. He had worked making sets for theatre and television: he knew how to tie knots and drive stakes, how to run power saws and hammer boards together, how to hook up lights and gas. He figured he could learn gardening and chicken coops and all the rest.

But he did not count on the kind of work available— or not available—in the country, or the kind of money the work paid. He did not count on his children needing to enroll in schools and needing also a way to get to those schools. He did not count on his family needing a place to call home that was not a tent or a makeshift trailer on a piece of borrowed land, with no water or heat or fridge, just a cooler with a block of ice and a camp stove and a Coleman lantern so we could read or play cards at night. My father did not factor in the character of country people, who were not necessarily up on the finer distinctions

between hippies and near-hippies, or between sun-dark-
ened Jews and plain-old Mexicans. He did not count on
the arguments and silences and despair hovering in the
air above our family, ready at any moment to ignite, like
the wildfires Californians are always so afraid of at the
end of summer, when the ground can't even remember
what rain feels like, and the shoreline of the lake recedes
daily, leaving pools of drying mud where water used to be.

Nor did he count on how important and how hard
it would be to teach his wife to drive—something she'd
never needed to know in the city. My father tried to
instruct my mother, but he got impatient and she became
even more birdlike than usual. He was infuriated that
she couldn't master the timing of the clutch and the gas
pedal, the steering and the brake, and how far away she
needed to be from the sides of the road. In the camper in
the back of the truck, we kids tried to ignore the sound of
our father yelling at our mother in the cab up front. The
air was hot and dry, like every day here in summer, and
the road was hard-packed gravel dusted with soft, cream-
colored dirt that flew in through the open windows and
coated our skin, our hair, our teeth. We didn't need the
intercom to know what was going on up front. The engine
whined and sputtered as our mom overturned the key,
overgunned the gas pedal. The truck crept forward, then
stopped with a jerk. Silence. The engine started up again.
The truck lunged, then coughed and spasmed. Saved by a
bit of gas, it rolled slowly, slowly. A screech of the brakes
told us we'd come to the end of the stretch of road. The
truck stalled again as my mother tried to turn it around.

My brothers and I read comic books and looked out the window at the oaks with their spiky leaves; the pale, brittle moss lacing up the tree trunks; the almond-colored dust covering everything. Every once in a while I'd sit up to look through the cab window to see my parents sitting in the wrong places on the wide bench seat, my father looking straight ahead, my mother glancing over at him. When my dad got angry at my mom like this, her head bobbed and her hands fluttered and her mouth either shut in a tight smile or muttered, "Sorry, sorry." It was one of the few things that could get us kids to stop yelling and squirming and shoving and leaning and pinching and breathing on each other. In the back of the truck, my brothers and I banded together in a kind of silent prayer, willing Mom to get it and Dad to stop being mad so she *could* get it.

A month later, on a clear October morning, my father finally gave up on his plan. That summer would be the first and only time I would witness him in the throes of optimism, in the act of trying to make a wish come true. When he failed, he seemed to swallow his hope along with his shame, and he never let either of them out again. We spent all morning packing up the truck, then waited till the heat of the day passed before starting back to the city.

We arrived between midnight and morning, both too late and too early to wake up the friends whose house we would stay at while we looked for yet another place to live. My dad parked on a hill, on a block with more empty lots than houses, under the branches of a huge metal radio tower. My mother climbed in the back with us, my father stretched out on the front seat, and the five of us slept until a cop banged his fist on the truck window to wake us up and tell us there was no camping on city streets and we had to move on.

CHAPTER 4
JUST KEEP NODDING AND AVOID THE TOPIC OF LAWNS

The next flat we moved into was big enough to have a bed-room for each kid, though we all envied my older brother, whose room was closest to the kitchen and the food. The apartment, which we could not afford, was located on the far edge of the Mission district right across from a park with a public swimming pool and a huge cypress tree that I once climbed up but could not climb down. We were just down the block from the housing projects, where heavy metal fire doors led to cement stairwells wet with beer and mold and urine. A few blocks away was 24th street, with the Mexican bakeries, and Inez, a fellow fifth grader from my new school who wore her dark hair in two long braids every single day. Another girl from my class lived right on my street; Maria was from the Philip-pines, though her house was as lacy and clean and Catho-lic as Inez's. Her family said grace before they ate their fried noodles and *lumpia*, and her mother made the sign of a cross every time she got into a car.

My dad was making art, or craft, as he called it, out of wood that spun like a planet on a lathe, in a shop on an oily, crumbling pier on the bay—a pier that would eventually, like so many of them, go down in flames. But he was also now working for the signmakers and display union, carrying a toolbox into hotels and arenas, setting up booths for conventions and trade shows, and then taking them down three or four days later. My mother was finishing her associate's degree at the community college, and going into nursery schools to do her student teaching. And my brothers and I were making friends and mischief in our new neighborhood and new schools, where we had enrolled a month late.

San Francisco must have been a city full of children in 1972, because extra classrooms, in the form of prefabricated, puce-colored bungalows, sprouted up like fungus in schoolyards all over the city. My school was composed entirely of bungalows, maybe ten of them arranged in a square around an asphalt yard. It was an alternative public school, where fourth, fifth, and sixth graders all learned together in the same classes and called the teachers by their first names, and where the principal applied for grants for visiting artists and student-exchange programs. I was one of three white kids in my class; the others had parents or skin tones from Mexico, China, Africa, India, the Philippines, and possibly more countries as well. One day, our teachers walked us through the sunny streets of the lower Mission district to the auditorium we sometimes borrowed from a neighboring elementary school. Inside, the lights were low and a movie screen was set up. There may have been an introduction, but the artist-in-residence knew that the surest way to pique the attention of 200 ten-through-twelve-year-olds was just to roll the film. What we saw had no color, no sound except for some tinny old piano music, and the pictures were small and square. But Charlie Chaplin, in mustache and baggy trousers, waddled around like a duck on speed, challenging the big goons in the factory, getting hung up in the gears, and all of us in the room—students and teachers alike—forgot that just outside the thick stucco walls the sun was shining on wooden crates piled high with limes and peppers and mangos, cars were honking at each other and people were yelling at each other, and tufts of yellow sour grass buds were pushing themselves up through the cracks in the sidewalks.

One kid from each classroom got to be in the film-making project, and it was my fortune to be selected—though perhaps it was a misfortune to touch, at such an impressionable age, the dream-making machinery of a movie camera. Once a week the filmmaker came to our school, and five of us got excused from class to pile into his busted-up car with the camera and a few pieces of gear. We learned how to load the film cartridge into the hollow gut of the Super-8 camera, how to screw the camera onto the tripod and put one eye up to the little window that reduced the world to a small, manageable square, and then to pull the trigger, the quick tick-tick-tick of the film's sprockets grabbing onto metal wheels inside the camera and pulling itself past the lens.

Our movie was about a group of kids that gets in trouble at school, runs away, then gets chased all over San Francisco by a truant officer played by our cool art

teacher. In it, we run herky-jerky, Chaplin-style to all the
famous tourist attractions that in our real lives we rarely
went to see: the Golden Gate Park band shell, where we
dart in and out of the shadows of the stone pillars; the cir-
cular cable-car turnaround at Hyde Street, where we help
the grip man push the car around; the wax museum in
Fisherman's Wharf—getting in free, once again—where
we stand frozen among the statues of Dorothy and Toto
and the Tin Man. In the end, we play a dangerous game
of hide-and-seek at the Cliff House, among the decaying
pits of the once-grand, turn-of-the-century Sutro Baths,
only to save the life of the truant officer when he falls over
the cliffs with the landmark Seal Rock in the background.

The Peeky Boo Bunch Plays Hooky won the 1973
Kodak-Eastman Amateur Filmmaker Award, and local
and national news reporters came to interview me, as I was
the articulate one, apparently, of this film crew. One afternoon, producers from the city's news magazine program
sent their van to interview me in front of the Cliff House
where we had filmed our dramatic rescue scene. They fit
wires around my neck and then fluffed up my sweatshirt
to hide them. "Try to include my question in your answer,"
said the interviewer, a woman wearing a straight skirt and
makeup. We sat on a cement ledge with the Pacific Ocean
in the background and she asked me how we'd made the
shot where the truant officer dangles over the cliff.

"It was easy," I responded. Then I remembered what
she'd said about repeating the question in the answer. "It
was really easy to make that scene on the cliff look dangerous," I said.

The lady, dark hair, plum-colored lipstick, smiled and nodded her head.

"He was standing on a ledge, but you never see his feet." Pointing to the cliffs, I went into the details. We had put the camera above him, and focused on his hands gripping the rock and his face peering up in desperation.

The lady smiled and nodded again, or perhaps she had never stopped. She wanted dynamic footage and lots of sound bites and I was happy to comply. "Then we moved him to another spot, where he got down on the ground and just dangled his legs over the cliff," I explained. "We shot that from below."

I went on to make more films with that artist-in-residence, to work on other kids' movies, and to serve as a judge in student film contests. At that age, it did not yet occur to me to doubt myself, even in front of an auditorium full of education professionals who had been brought in to discuss the value of teaching filmmaking to school children, and even when one of the educators, annoyed by my ten-year-old confidence, tried to trip me up with a question.

"You mentioned the 'editing process' a couple times," she said, leaning toward me from her seat in the audience. She sounded sort of like the television interviewer, like she didn't quite believe I had done what I'd done, but she wanted to hear me talk about it anyway. "Can you tell us what, exactly, you mean by 'editing'?"

"Oh, editing is when you go through all the film you shot and take out the bad stuff and put all the good stuff together so it makes sense," I replied, unaware of her hostility until the filmmaker-in-residence boasted about it later, and likewise unaware of the self-satisfied smirks on the faces of the other teachers who watched me answer her with a straight face, as if I were helping out a slow child.

Moviemaking is witchcraft and trickery, making people see and believe things that aren't really there. With no equipment other than a super-8 camera on a tripod, and one light, also on a tripod, we were able to make our *Peeky Boo* bunch run double fast, dangle over ocean cliffs, disappear in the aisles of Walgreens as we rubbed on "vanishing cream." We made a semester's worth of afternoons look like one day by keeping our hair trimmed and wearing (except when we forgot) the same T-shirts and jeans each time. Later, we learned animation, and how to make cardboard creatures walk, run, and fly with the help of a few swivel clips in their joints and a push button on the end of a cable release so we could expose only one, two, or three frames at a time. And at the little super-8 editor, we cut one piece of film and taped it to another to construct scenes and to jump—pow—between scenes to move the story along.

When that artist-in-residence put the small box of a camera into our hands, he gave us the opportunity to write the world rather than just read it. He gave us the chance to change the very shape of the universe, to make like Charlie Chaplin and climb inside the gears of the machine and wreak havoc. He gave us the chance to see— for there is no clarity like that which appears in the view-finder of a camera—and then to project that vision to the world. And then, finally, to view ourselves projected up there on a screen, as if we were as real as James Bond or Superfly or Batman.

We also got the chance to go, with other filmmaking kids from our school, on an exchange program to a school in Southern California. It was an inner-city to suburbs exchange, and I was the only white girl representing my school, though I'm not sure I realized it at the time. I was too busy ironing the red-and-navy cotton jacket my mother had made for me, packing up my new instamatic, and boarding my first airplane for the seventy-five-minute flight into another world. At the airport in L.A., perky mothers in station wagons picked us up and brought us to the school, which impressed us city kids for the sheer amount of grass that surrounded it. Then we got divvied up and introduced to our host families, more perky moms and their kids, and the whole lot of us rendezvoused at Universal Studios.

On the studio tour, we witnessed more ways to make tricks with film, such as granite boulders made out of light-weight foam for easy lifting, and back-screens showing footage of the river flowing behind the bow of the African Queen. But it was back at my host family's home that night that I really felt like I was walking around on a sound stage.

It was late afternoon when we drove up to their house, a sprawling rectangle surrounded on all four sides by lawn which sloped, like a kelly-green sea, up to a foundation demarcated by neatly trimmed hedges and flower beds—a scene as pristine and lifeless as any of the

movie sets we'd visited at Universal Studios. We parked in
a driveway in front of a garage, and though I tried so hard
to shut the car door gently, it reverberated awkwardly
in the silence of this so-called neighborhood that was
composed only of houses and lawns—no corner stores,
no traffic lights, no schoolyard, no streetcars or streetcar tracks, no bus stops, no busses to stop. There were
all kinds of doors into this house, but we walked up the
driveway to a little path that crossed a corner of that magnificent grass ocean and into a side entrance. The mom
led me down a carpeted hall to my room; it was an extra
room whose sole purpose was to house people like me,
guests, and otherwise went empty. I put my cloth jacket
and my instamatic on the dresser and then sat on the bed,
listening to the sound of all that unused space.

Dinner was served at a table and in a room reserved
just for eating dinner, as opposed to the breakfast table in
the kitchen alcove, which was for eating breakfast. Where
did they eat lunch, I had to wonder, but didn't dare ask.
The father was home, now, too, and he sat at the head of
the table in a suit and tie, picking up dishes and offering
them around. The topic of conversation—I couldn't help
but bring it up—was the lawn. And the father, in between
bites and swallows, asked me, in turn, about the yard at
my house.

Where I come from, I explained while dishes got
passed and spoonfuls got served onto plates, some people
did have lawns in front of their houses, but my own house,
which was actually just the top floor of a house, did not
have a front lawn, as the sidewalk and the stoop and the

landing with the three doors to the first-floor, second-floor, and third-floor flats took up the space where any grass might grow. And the mom and the dad and the kids sitting around the table in the house with the lawn all smiled and nodded to each other and to me. And then we all took another bite of meat, and we chewed and smiled again, and the father added, "So you do your gardening in the *back* yard."

And I knew enough, even then, just to keep nodding, to let them think what they wanted to—it's easier and more comfortable on everyone that way—rather than telling them the truth, which was that there was neither yard, nor lawn, in the back, either.

Back home from Southern California, I watched my parents retreating into their own corners, my father silent or yelling, my mother silent or singing to herself, a secret smile spreading across her face. Across town, Ronald Reagan, then governor of the state, was sending National Guard troops to beat up the students at San Francisco State, the very college my mother dreamed of attending. Elsewhere in the city, the Zodiac killer was still wandering around and Patty Hearst was either willingly or under coercion—will we ever really know for sure?—helping the Symbionese Liberation Army to rob banks, kill people, and feed the poor. The sweet stench of pot smoke was rising up from playgrounds and parked cars, and on my street corner, black men from the projects stood on a carpet of broken glass harmonizing soul songs that sounded even better than the radio.

"Money money money money, money.
Money money money money, money.
Some people, got to have it;
Some people, really need it…"

The argument at home was, as always, about where to go next. My mother wanted to move back to the state college's student housing project in the city's foggy hinterlands, where we had lived when I was a baby and my father was finishing up his humanities degree. Mom's confidence was just gaining on her—this was the force behind that smile—as she'd come to realize that she, too, could go to college, as had her husband, as had many, many other people she knew and did not know. The rent was cheap at State's campus housing, and she could walk to classes, just as my father had done when it was his turn to be a college student. But now, my father resisted. Perhaps he had other reasons, but the one I kept overhearing was about size: the college's two-bedroom apartments were too small for our family of five.

It was a good point. We'd been out to see those converted army barracks covered with gray asphalt shingles, the sand pit that passed for a playground, the rickety stairwells that housed four identical units, two on the first floor and two on the second. It was a gray foggy afternoon, and even without furniture, the living room felt crowded with all five of us standing in it. From inside the front door, we could see every corner of the rest of the apartment: the kitchen, just big enough for our rectangular table if we pushed it up against the wall; the bedroom my parents would share; the bedroom my brothers would share; the closet that my father could maybe turn into a bedroom for me.

There was a scuffle between one brother and me, a thump and a hiss, an elbow to a back, a knee to a thigh. I ran for the bathroom, like I always did, because back at our house, it was the only door with a lock. Whizzing past my parents and through the doorway, I pivoted around to slam the bathroom door and set the lock in one fell swoop. But my hands came up empty: this door did not have a lock, just a loose metal doorknob spinning in my palm. My brothers, now teaming up against me, laughed at my astonishment, and then simply leaned until the door gave way and they could get at me.

A month later we were living in those four meager rooms, though size, it turns out, was only one of the problems the new house promised us.

CHAPTER 5
DON'T FEED THE ROACHES

When my father built my bed and wedged it into an over-sized closet flanked by the two real bedrooms, he probably had no idea about the cockroaches, how they would come to see this bed—or at least the places where its posts nudged up against the walls and ceiling—as their very own. He called it a Dutch bed; it sat up high, like the top of a bunk bed, but instead of another bed below it there was a little dresser and a mirror on one side, and a little desk on the other. A curtain hung down from the bed, pretending to be the door to the closet that was pretending to be my room. From my perch, I could see and hear everything in the flat. I could smell dinner and know who was in the bathroom. I could tell my brothers to be quiet, turn down the TV, turn off the lights—I'm trying to sleep. And I could gaze at the roaches meandering in and out of the gaps between wood and plaster, hatching eggs, shedding their casings, waving their antennae out in front of them as if swaying to gospel music.

The first thing to know about cockroaches is that they eat paper. At night, in my loft, I'd marvel at how the roaches could squeeze themselves into those cracks between the wood and the plaster. My strategy was to suffocate them by shoving crumpled-up newspaper into their breathing space. But it turned out I was feeding them, like you might feed your gerbils or goldfish. They accepted the paper wads with greed and gratitude, and treated me friendly in return. Throughout the apartment, instead of scurrying when we threw on a light or opened a drawer, they just moseyed along, startled, a bit annoyed. The cockroaches acted like they owned the place—and indeed they did—while the humans in the house learned to check and shake everything, to rinse the dishes before using them, to make sure there were no little surprises piggy-backing to school with us in our coats or book bags. In the kitchen, you had to watch out, especially with the spices; better just to toss them all in the garbage, since those tiny dark eggs are so easily camouflaged as grains of nutmeg or black pepper.

I watched my father make that closet into a room. It took maybe a week. I was in sixth grade now, and supposed to be at my new school, but I didn't like it there: it was too stern and suburban, too white, after my open classroom of the year before. Plus, I could feel something brewing between my parents, some storm unlike the others we'd weathered. There had been less arguing, but also less talking in general.

So I just stayed home, and as long as I was quiet and didn't ask questions, my dad didn't say anything either. He let me watch him work, probably assuming I was learning something just as valuable as what they were teaching at school. Yellow pencil behind his ear, tape measure in his hands, sawdust on his face and his hair, he fitted fleshy pink two-by-fours into the corners, then put the plywood on top, two feet from the ceiling. More two-by-fours, cut into short segments, made a ladder up one side, and then he added a tall shelf on the other side. It was ingenious, really—this square cubby with its nest of a bed—though it provided me no room to grow. When we put the foam rectangle on the plywood to try it out, I had to lie on the diagonal to keep my head and feet from pressing up against the walls.

Everyone else was at school—my mother, my brothers, all the neighbors—and the house was silent except for sawing and hammering, the pouring of coffee and cream, the dissolving of sugar as the teaspoon rang against the ceramic walls of the cup. The handsaw went on with a sharp tang, then slowed to a grunt as it moved through the wood, leaving the sweet smell of sawdust in its wake. A slight "damn" escaped from my father's lips, scooting around his cigarette. He slid the pencil from behind his ear, made another mark, then picked up the saw again.

Did he already know he would be leaving? Bam, bam, bam, bam on the hammer, and the nail disappeared. Was it the house, the too-small size of it and the too-far-away of it that made him mad about moving there? Or was he still fuming about the fact that he couldn't make his moving-to-the-country dream come true? Could he tell, even before we moved across town to the outskirts of the city, back to the university's student housing, that this place would divorce our family? He pounded the last nail into the wood so that only its flat metal head was visible. As soon as that bed was made, he seemed to be gone.

When we lived there the first time, back when we were just a family of four and my father was finishing his degree, it was still called Married Student Housing. In the pictures of me there, it's sunny, I am a baby in a flouncy dress, sitting up, proud and happy, then crawling toward my three-year-old big brother and the apple he is eating. The barracks in the background seem benign; there are no signs of cockroaches. The sky is clear and the day is warm and my legs are bare, my feet open to the sun and the air.

Now, as an almost-teenager with my parents not talking to each other, it seemed perpetually chilly, shrouded in fog. The picture we have from this second time shows my younger brother and my father, who is a visitor at this point, grim and smiling on a peeling-paint stairwell. An old wooden sewing machine box sits in the corner of the porch, and an abandoned bike lock dangles from the railing. Now there were more single parents than married ones, so the university called this place Family Student Housing instead of Married Student Housing. Those of us who lived there called it Gatorville. The name came from the college's football team, the Gators—as in Golden Gate Bridge—who played in the field next to us.

Our buildings sat in a fog-filled basin at the bottom of a hill, far away from stores and schools and other neighborhoods. In addition to the football field, we were bordered by a five-story parking garage and a long hill up to the shopping center and the buses that could pick you up and take you to the rest of the city located somewhere out there. But our isolated valley neighborhood was immersed in salty ocean air and the moist menthol of eucalyptus, a combination of smells that will always make me feel sad and at home.

A dozen buildings arched around two streets, one straight and one curved, so that from the hill above they made the shape of a capital D. Each building had three stairwells, and each stairwell had two apartments downstairs and two upstairs. A narrow catwalk along the upper back doors allowed for all kinds of mischief, including spying on people in the bathroom and listening, crouched low, to dinner conversations. The apartments were all exactly the same, but most looked better than ours. We had a table and three chairs—my dad took the other two—in the kitchen, and a foam mattress sitting on the floor in the living room in front of a little black-and-white TV that was sitting on a crate.

The kids in Gatorville outnumbered the adults by two or three to one. There were dozens and dozens of us, and we were for the most part unruly and unrulable. What laws there were got set by the oldest boys and then followed or broken—if we dared—by the rest of us. The parents were exhausted from going to college and working jobs to pay for college, and they had no time or energy left to control their children. They could barely get us fed and dressed, the crumbs wiped off our faces, a comb run through the knots in our hair. The air in that damp little canyon was tinged with wildness, with mutiny. It was something like a prison where the inmates have taken over, though not everything we did was mean. At the community center, we did batik and tie-dye, and started a neighborhood newspaper which we supported with spaghetti feeds. My brothers and their friends made more money than any of us had ever seen by singing Christmas carols one December in the outdoor shopping mall up the hill. We set up plywood scraps on the speed bumps in our U-shaped street, and spent hours practicing tricks on our bikes and skateboards with no interruptions from cars.

Once, the older boys dug a hole in the playground behind our back steps. They passed around a couple shovels, my older brother and four others, and they just started digging. They had no time to be home by. They went back for food and flashlights and they dug all night long and into the dawn. They dug until there was no more sand but dirt, and then they dug the dirt until there was nothing left that shovels could dig. It was a kind of infinity they had dug into, invigorating rather than frightening, and they stood, all five of them, in their giant hole, and beamed as if they had conquered Everest.

Apparently my mother, caught in her own brazen fit of optimism, had decided that it would be better to do everything—school, work, raising children—on her own. She never explained to us kids exactly why she filed for divorce, though there must have been a family meeting in which the word came down that she and my father would no longer be arguing and making up. But there is no dramatic scene to explain the moment the marriage finally went awry, no caustic event that severed the family from itself. A divorce, after all, is not really a thing so much as the absence of a thing, like weather or gravity, that you never knew could not exist.

My guess is that my mother had grown tired of feeling like something was wrong with her and that she had become seduced by the glamour of independence and the promise of happiness that it held. Now that she was enrolled at the university she had accomplished one of her dreams and—for a brief moment—was infected with the power of possibility. The rest of us did not know what hit us.

For me, it was an introduction to impulsiveness. Probably my mother had made sudden decisions before, and it was probably these decisions, emerging from her deep urge to break out of her confines, that had caused my dad to call her names. But this time, I was old enough, eleven, to notice her eyes widen in some combination of presumption and doubt as she took a giant leap forward, trying to defy her arid history and all those bad things her mother and husband had told her about herself. She smiled, she danced, she sang. She radiated with potency. But it was a vigor based on wishing, which has such trouble holding itself up. She wasn't thinking about consequences; she was acting on an impulse—a noble one, to rid herself of shackles, but, like all impulses, subject to regret.

Once, a few months after she made her decision, my mother and I were walking to the supermarket. My dad had the truck, and my mom had neither a car nor a license; she didn't know how to drive, as my father had not been able to teach her about the clutch and the gas pedal on those dusty roads in the country just two years earlier. It took a good half hour to walk up the hill out of Gatorville to the shopping center to get groceries, which we'd then shove into our backpacks for the walk back home. Some days we were lucky enough to sneak a shopping cart out of the parking lot, load it up with our bags, and ride it all the way down the hill back home.

It was evening when we walked up the hill, the time just after sunset that photographers call magic hour— though it really only lasts a few minutes—when the sky turns from one shade of ephemeral, metallic blue to the next. My mother may have had a touch of liquor; she never drank, but she was trying all sorts of new things lately.

"Do you think I made a mistake?" she asked me.

"About what?" I said, though I knew what she was referring to.

"Your father. The divorce."

We could not see each other well; the light was disappearing from the air around us, and we were walking profile to profile. Plus, we knew how each other looked: she had light eyes and a broad forehead, long, thin hair parted down the middle, and I looked too much like her. But the sound of her voice—full of air and worry, a flute being played by someone who couldn't blow right—told me I had to provide comfort.

"Oh, no, Mom. It was the right thing to do."

My father, meanwhile, was so surprised and so furious that his anger no longer fit into words or gestures,
and he simply shut up. He had tried to do the right thing,
to marry and work and support his accidental family even
though he himself had once harbored dreams of becoming a professor or a craftsman or a philosopher. For the
sake of his children and his wife, he had given up on his
own dreams of artistry, independence, and finding Land,
and had taken a union job, setting up conventions downtown and then tearing them down. The woman he married was a little childlike in her giddiness and neediness,
the way she needed to be reminded—or did she?—of the
most commonsense things. But he'd fallen for her and
faced the consequences. Then in one impulsive swoop,
it was all over and out of his control. He left the house,
stopped talking to my mother, and began to communicate to her through us, the children, who at that time
were eight, eleven, and thirteen. It turns out my father
had his own childish side, as he was unable to push his
pain out of the way in order to help his children make the
best of things. Also, like my mother, he never seemed to
fully comprehend the enormous sway that they, simply
by being parents, held in the lives of their children. They
employed a hands-off approach partly because it was
all they could manage, and partly, I think, because they
believed it was the way for us to create our own relationship with the world.

Every once in a while, however, my father would sit
us down and try to teach us a lesson. Once, before he'd
moved out of Gatorville, the cops came knocking on our

door. They were investigating a break-in, and were looking for some friends of my older brother's who may have
smashed a window and climbed into a neighbor's house.
My parents were polite but reserved. They didn't know
where those boys lived, they told the two officers who
seemed to fill our small living room with their black and
their shine: jackets, badges, belts, hats, and even guns. But
I knew.

"I can show you where they live," I chirped up, and
pointed out the way.

After the bulky uniforms left, my parents tried to
explain to me how the good guys weren't always so good,
and the bad guys weren't always bad.

"It's best to say as little as possible around the police,"
my dad said.

"Isn't that lying?" I asked.

"Not exactly," he said. His voice was soft and deliberate, and he was squinting his eyes like he did when he was
concentrating on an idea or a piece of artwork. "It's just
not going out of our way to help them out."

"We don't want to help them?"

"Well, sometimes they're not really on our side," my
mother offered.

"But breaking into someone's house is definitely
bad," I said. "Right?"

"Yes," my father said. "But the police are not necessarily the best people to take care of that problem. They
can get those boys in a lot of trouble."

"Oh," I said, and looked away from him to the floor.
I remembered those uniformed officers that I'd seen on

TV attacking students on this very campus, and the cop who'd pulled my dad over once when we were in the truck and threatened to take him in because his breath smelled like pot. "I get it," I said, full of guilt.

Their united front did not last much longer, and my father slipped out of the house without a fuss; I don't even remember the day he left. Then, some months later, my older brother moved out as well. It wasn't a formal custody agreement. It was just that one day, instead of going to school, he'd taken the three busses to my dad's apartment, a one-room studio on a sunny hill with canneries and warehouses and artists' lofts, not too far from the city's industrial waterfront. I did not see my brother crouching in the bushes outside my father's studio on a steep concrete hill. I did not see him waiting for hours, his blue knit cap pulled down low, his jacket zipped up tight, nor my father parking the truck like a T into the curb so it wouldn't roll down the hill, slamming the heavy white door, then clomping up the wooden stairs in his brown-on-brown leather work boots. I did not see the rocks flying from the pile my brother had collected, smacking against the side of the house and the glass of the wide back window that looked out on the brewery, the tomato cannery, and the giant Coca-Cola sign flashing its red and white lights. Nor did I see my father, puzzled, then concerned, opening the back door, stepping onto the shady deck slick with fog and mildew, peering out through the leaves of the acacia tree, to find his brown-haired son, arm cocked, taking aim.

But apparently he disarmed my brother and got him inside, and from then on they shared that studio apartment, two single beds and a TV and fold-up kitchen table all in one room. And some time after that—I was eleven—I climbed down from my cockroach nest in the center of the Gatorville house and started sleeping in my mother's bed with her. My excuse was the roaches, and the fact that even if I slept on the diagonal, the walls pressed in on me from top and bottom, threatening to stunt my growth. But clearly it was also solace that caused me to move into my mother's bed. What's not so clear is *whose* solace—hers or mine—motivated this move.

While my parents were trying to right themselves, us kids were doing the same, entertaining ourselves with whatever we could find, steal, or make on our own. One afternoon a bunch of us kids in Gatorville took a shopping cart that had made its way down our hill from the grocery store, and pushed it up the slanted concrete floors of the five-story parking garage that was our closest neighbor. Two kids stayed below, as lookouts.

"All clear?" we shouted from the top of the garage, peering over the concrete wall. A minute passed, then another, as some grown-up scurried by below us. We scootched back from the edge, out of sight, and waited. "All clear?" we asked again, a bit more hesitantly, as we approached the edge once more.

"All clear," yelled the two lookouts, their faces pointed up at us like sunflowers.

It took four of us to hoist the cart up to the lip of the

cement wall and then shove it over the edge. We couldn't see anything below, and we hoped there were no cars or people in the way. It took an amazingly long and quiet time for the cart to reach the ground; it seemed almost to float, like a kite, and for a second we forgot how heavy it was.

Then it crashed, steel on asphalt, with a force—we knew from the noise—that could kill a person if they happened to be walking by. Pieces of metal and plastic flew off, and the carcass lay mangled and still, even as the noise continued bouncing off the concrete walls. We ran down the flights of stairs, took a look at the damage, and then, before anyone came investigating, scurried around collecting the loose parts and hauling the remains into the bushes.

It was the wheels, as well as the danger, that we were after. We needed to nail them to chunks of worn-gray two-by-fours and then to a slat of plywood. Then we added ropes to each side of the front axle to steer the thing, and a thick branch off a eucalyptus tree wedged at an angle in the rear as some kind of maybe brake. We built it in the bushes, with tools snuck out of our houses, and we covered it up each night with leaves and branches as camouflage.

The groups were always changing, depending on the project and who could contribute, but on this one we had maybe four boys and two girls, including me. After a week we took it out for a test drive, and then our group grew, as all the kids wanted to try it out, or at least see it go. But first they had to do their duty as lookouts. We went back to the garage, pulling the go-cart up the sloping concrete. Kids were stationed up, down, and over, watching for cars, people, and especially campus security, who, rumor had it, could arrest you just like the police could. Then we took turns flying down, wiping out on the turns, and trying to avoid the spiked treads at the bottom of the garage set out to discourage cars from sneaking out without paying.

We used to play a game, the whole neighborhood, except for the littlest kids. Word would go out late in the afternoon—*Whippersnappers tonight*—and then, as the sky darkened, kids would show up at the laundry house to get divvied up. The game was a combination of Nazi war criminals and western outlaws, a cross between *Hogan's Heroes* and *Wild, Wild West*, but us kids provided the laugh tracks, as well as the screams. The laundry house served as the prison and command center.

It was the older boys against the rest of us. They'd take towels from the dryers and clothes from the free box, roll them up into weapons, then snap them at you. It could sting enough to bring tears to your eyes, especially if they used jeans, with their metal buttons and zippers. If they snapped you, they could then drag you to jail, where you sat on washing machines—your cells—and tried to engineer a diversion and escape out the back window. The guard could make you do whatever he wanted: lick the floor, tie his shoes, repeat humiliating statements about yourself or your mother. He got a menacing gleam in his eye that you could see even in the dark. He hit you with a fierce snap of a towel, sharp and loud, and if you cried he'd do it again. Those who complained or disobeyed or told their parents were not allowed to play, and everyone wanted to play. There was no winning or losing. There was just the thrill of fear and torture and escape.

And then there was another game, of sorts. I played it with a girl my age, almost twelve, who lived out of the neighborhood, a streetcar ride away, and was rougher and more experienced than I was, though her mother and stepfather were also sort-of hippies. She was a dark-skinned white girl with long black hair as if maybe her dad—who lived in some other state—was Indian. She taught me how to smoke cigarettes, and how to take a razor blade and carve a boy's initials in my skin, down by the ankles, so they'd scab over like a tattoo. Our game was passing out. You could do it with or without smoking pot. One person would hyperventilate and then hold her breath, while another would push her hands, hard, against your chest. You'd wake up on the ground a minute or two later, with everyone standing over you, laughing. We did it outside on a dry grassy hill, with the smell of wild anise in the air, or inside a bedroom when the mom wasn't home; sometimes just the two of us, sometimes three or four or five of us.

My friend had two sisters, older, always getting grounded. She knew the drawer where they hid an envelope that held tiny squares, like pieces of clear glitter. "It's just like getting stoned, only more," she told me, folding two of those tabs into a piece of paper and slipping it into the front pocket of her jeans.

We ate the little squares on a Gatorville community

field trip. It was blustery and cold, and we were driving in someone's van, a bunch of us kids piled into the seats. The acid had a crunch to it. How could this thin little flake do anything to a human body? It was as small and see-through as a fish scale off the bluegills we'd caught at Clear Lake. I had read about LSD, about everything you always wanted to know about sex, about Sybil and Alice, about the way prisoners could get high with nutmeg. I'd read Agatha Christie and *Charlie and the Chocolate Factory* and *The Lion, the Witch and the Wardrobe*, too. I was a curious eleven-year-old and often alone; my father was gone and my mother was usually out. I read a lot, but I did not know that acid was another name for LSD.

When the drug started coming on, we had climbed out of the van and were walking around on a long, curved cement fishing pier where Filipino families huddled around poles and lines and ice chests filled with cokes and bait. The pier started erupting as if it were a roller coaster, and I had trouble staying on it. Then we got back into the van and I sat close to the front, near the driver, amazed by everything he did to make the vehicle go, astounded by the oncoming cars, with their headlights on against the dark-gray fog.

We got to the picnic spot and unloaded the van. I waited in line for a long time for my hot dog, but then when I got it I had no interest in it. I wanted the swings, and then I just wanted to go home, to undo whatever I had done. I could not find any words to describe what was happening and so I just laughed or cried instead. I was afraid people would find out what I had taken, so I pretended I had a stomachache and would throw up if I talked.

When I finally got home, my mother was not there. She was rarely there; my brothers and I seemed to be so good at taking care of ourselves that she thought she wasn't needed. She spent her time in class or at work or at a poetry reading or a dance recital, and sometimes she brought us along so we too could get infected with excitement. She was now full of a brand-new confidence, glowing with ideas and throbbing with the gusto to carry them out. She was liberated and exuberant—perhaps too exuberant?—studying, working as a campus landscaper, running the projector at the student film series, writing poems and publishing them in thin paperback anthologies. She was banishing all sense of "no" that she had received from her mother and her husband and everyone else in the world. She was opening cans of paint, and making quick, bold stripes of gold and russet and tangerine on the wall in her bedroom, and then running off to do the next thing.

I got into her bed, which was also kind of my bed, and stared at those bright autumn colors as they walked away from the wall and twisted themselves into swirls and curves and tangled round shapes that kept morphing into other tangled round shapes. The drug was finally wearing off, and I was relieved to know that this thing was ending, that I would not be stuck there in that convoluted fright forever. My brother and I lay down on the red patchwork quilt on my mother's bed and played Chutes and Ladders—that's how young he still was and I was only three

years older—and he took every advantage of my distracted state of mind to steal paces, re-roll the dice, take
extra turns. He knew I was sick, so he had to take care of
me, but that didn't mean he wasn't going to beat me at
the game while he had the chance. I stared into his green
eyes, so like my own but a little happier, and saw worry,
confusion, and intrigue. He didn't know what was going
on, but he knew something was going on. And the same
could be said for me.

Chapter 6
Send for the Helicopter

This is how I always imagined it would happen. A helicopter buzzes into the vicinity of 16th and Sanchez, which will forever be my home no matter how many times we move away. It circles, as if searching for someone among the kids playing in the schoolyard, the people waiting for green lights to replace red ones, and the guys walking out of the corner store tapping packs of cigarettes against their palms. A megaphone-voice booms down from the 'copter. "You there," it says, as if it were God or at least a voice-over narrator. All earthly activity comes to a halt as we look around at each other wondering who he's talking to. "Yes, you," the voice says again, and I realize that it is me they have come for; they have come for me at last. A rope ladder drops down. "Come on up," the announcer says. And I start climbing that swaying ladder, till my block, the school, the corner store all shrink into nothingness, till everything about normal life—all the regular working and out-of-work people with their lives restricted by money and physics and anonymity—is far below me. "Welcome aboard," says 'copter man, handing me my gear and leading me to my seat.

Then off we go to a kind of Paris-salon-in-the-clouds peopled with creative geniuses on par with Pablo Picasso or Miles Davis—bold, brilliant, complicated people glossy with vitality and accomplishment; artists and musicians and writers and philosophers and filmmakers and revolutionaries who are routinely excused for their eccentricities and bad behavior, people who are doing things with words and music and paint and film that have never been done before and that will change the way they are done forever after. Like many girls my age, I start out with an infatuation with David Cassidy. But as I and the fantasy age, the cast changes as well, and by the time I finish college it includes Maya Angelou and Ernie Kovacs, Dorothy Parker, Malcolm X, Robert Altman, Bob Dylan, and Spike Lee—an odd collection of characters living and dead all gathered together as if they were on Steve Allen's old *Meeting of the Minds* show. These are the people who matter, the ones who are probing for the very truth of the world. And I slip into the hot, white circle of fame, assuming my rightful place among them.

At first the dream serves a purpose: It saves your life. You have discovered that the world is not based on merit, but is split arbitrarily into two zones, the zone of abundance and the zone of want. In other words, you are a Have Not in a world constructed not *by* but *for* people who Have. You also know that nothing—not the planet suspended in gravity, not your home or parents—can be depended upon. And as you walk around the neighborhood with these ugly truths eating like battery acid at your insides, the dream of a helicopter escape keeps your hopes alive. "Don't worry," it coos. "I'll get you out of here." It allows you to tolerate the present, buoying your spirit with promise, so you can continue doing what you have to do—getting up in the morning and pouring the milk over the cereal, coming home in the afternoon to do your schoolwork at that same table, holding your mother's place in lines at welfare and unemployment, stuffing newspaper into cockroach nests up in the corners of the Dutch bed. My dream tantalized, gave me a whiff of the optimism and invincibility that get bestowed mostly on those who are born with money. It tricked me into thinking that I could erase my origins and just helicopter over to wherever I wanted to go. While in the throes of the fame fantasy, I became one of those who feel, and thus *are*, entitled to have or do whatever they desire, who believe that the world is open and waiting for them and all they have to do is help themselves to it.

In Gatorville, when I thought about the past—Clear Lake, 16th and Sanchez—I'd wonder how those times could seem so perfect and so sad at the same time. Just a couple years earlier, we'd been playing early-morning gangsters at a campground on the shore of a warm and shallow lake. Us kids had been a threesome and our family, despite its arguing, had an of-course-ness to it that seemed unbreakable. I had leaned back into my mother's arms in the water and I'd loved the feeling of being let go. Now my family was like a hand with five fingers: we were connected through anatomy but moved independently from each other, developing our own private lives, keeping our thoughts to ourselves, cooking and eating alone rather than around a table together. The children were still young, but so, also, were the parents. They were caught up in the pain (my father's) and exhilaration (my mother's) of the divorce. Somehow they forgot all they knew about weaning, about how crucial it is to ease the hands out slowly from underneath the child as she learns to float on her own, to stand nearby in case she starts to panic or sink. It's that abrupt release which forces the child to hold herself up by any means necessary. It leads her to jump over huge portions of childhood and teeter awkwardly between pleasures and dangers way beyond her years.

But mostly I was not thinking about the past, or even the present. I was dreaming of the future, a time and place that was, in my fantasy, as golden and wispy as the afterlife or a scene from a movie: impossible to believe in, but impossible to live without.

The winter I was eleven, the older Gatorville kids formed a flag football team, with a real coach, a chubby black man who showed up with yellow strips of fabric that we shoved down our pants and let dangle along our thighs. The flags were to keep us from tackling each other and grinding our bodies into the grass, which poked out bright and green from the dark, wet sod. It was all boys, except me, small and slight, thin messy hair turning from blonde to brown. But I could run, I could bump, I could even catch that fat brown egg of a ball—with two hands, hugging it like a baby into my belly and then hustling for the line. After a few weeks of playing around on the edge of the college team's practice field, our coach organized a game with another team in another part of town. And so one afternoon, my brothers and their friends and me—a mix of Mexicans and whites and one Korean kid—took a bus, then transferred to another, before landing on a patch of grass and dirt in a city park we didn't recognize. We had no uniforms, though we all tried to wear the same color T-shirt.

The other team had one girl as well. She was bigger than me by far. She was black, as was the rest of her team. Naturally the coaches matched the two girls, so she covered me and I covered her. The teams lined up facing each other, and we bent our knees and raised our heads toward each other. Her face was inches from mine, and she beat me with just her stare, her deep brown eyes penetrating into my earthy green ones yet somehow not seeing me at all.

"Sixteen! Thirty-seven! Twenty-four!" shouted our center. Then, "Hike!"

He snapped the ball, and the two teams rushed towards each other. I tried to find a hole, but my man, who was this girl, was all over me. Everywhere I went, there she was, nudging me in all the legal ways, but working me over just the same. She kept her hands to her sides, but lowered her shoulders into mine, pushing me backward. She shoved a knee between my legs, and when I lost my balance, she stuck her chest out and bumped me till I toppled over. Meanwhile, the ball was passed, the catch was dropped, the backs and the ends were running after each other.

Finally a whistle blew, and we reformed into our lines. On each play, I got a bit better at dodging her, but I never made any forward gains. Neither of us ever touched the ball—just each other—but we had our own battle on the field, and I got a glimpse of a different degree of anger, of an anger that rages against all the unfairnesses by slamming itself into a human body over and over again. I can't remember which team won the game, but I remember not caring about the outcome, just wanting it to be over.

My older brother played on the flag football team and went on to play football in high school. But generally, visits with him and with my father had to be arranged by telephone and were awkward when they happened: we went bowling, or to the movies, instead of just hanging out in our pajamas reading comic books or watching Saturday morning cartoons, alternately yelling and laughing. My own anger, when not turned against my mother and brothers, went dormant, so I could carry on and do the things I had to do, such as stealing cigarettes and hanging around boys who stole cars or putting my clothes in the washer at the Laundromat, then running up the hill to the grocery store for a package of fish sticks and frozen potatoes, which I'd cook up for dinner for my little brother and or he'd cook up for me. (My brothers and I had a gruff, silent way of stepping in to parent each other.)

One gray foggy afternoon, I sat on the bare floor of an abandoned apartment in one of the barracks with a group of twelve- and thirteen-year-olds and a bottle we were spinning around. All of the kids were from our neighborhood, except one guy—older, at fourteen—who

went to the junior high school with one of our teenagers, and liked hanging in Gatorville because you could
get away with so much here. We'd broken into the apartment, which was between renters, through a window in
the back. Then we sat in a circle and began twirling the
bottle. My dare was to go into the closet with the older
boy and let him do whatever he wanted. I wasn't one to
back down from a dare—especially when the alternative
was to reveal something about myself—and so I stood up
and followed him as he opened the door, pulled me in,
and closed it behind us.

What he wanted was to wedge my lips open with his
tongue, and then swish it around the inside of my mouth.
What he wanted was to grope at the small mounds growing on my chest, to let his hands take a cursory trip
around the crotch of my jeans, and then to lean his whole
body into mine with a few quick, meaningless thrusts,
both of us standing up, fully clothed. The darkness made
the small square of a closet, which was empty except for
a few bare clothes hangers dangling above us, seem like it
went on forever. My eyes, if he could have seen them, were
staring off into that black space. My skin, if he'd taken a
moment to feel it, was calcifying once again, the soft, pliant cells hardening into those of an old, jaded woman. I
was in sixth grade and had never French kissed before,
but it was just like everything else I knew about sex and
men: slimy and insistent. They thought they were getting
inside you, but they didn't realize—or didn't care—that
you were all closed up, sealed off from everything.

—

In Gatorville, eviction hovered once again. The university wanted to tear down the whole family student housing project and offer nothing in its stead. The reasons were commonplace and plentiful: the buildings were unsafe and the college couldn't afford to upgrade them; the parking lot needed to be expanded; budgets were getting cut and funding was running out. The usual excuses and explanations. The community started holding meetings, talking to pro-bono lawyers, writing letters, staging small protests with hand-painted placards in front of the college offices.

My parents had taken us on long marches against the Viet Nam War, so my brothers and I knew about holding up signs and chanting with a large group of people. Now we found ourselves with a crowd of maybe fifty, mostly Gatorville residents plus a few students who would come out for any picket line taking place on campus. The fog made this southwestern strip of San Francisco perpetually chilly, so we were wearing sweatshirts with hoods, the drawstrings pulled tight around our chins. "Hell no, we won't go," we shouted joyously, our voices ringing with sweet determination, as we walked in a large circle in front of the administration building. There were dozens of kids in the group, and we thought it was fun to have a common enemy, to point up to the window where that enemy, the president of the university, was sitting behind his big, shiny desk, trying to ignore us. A reporter from the campus paper took our quotes and our pictures. We smiled and waved our signs as if we were at a baseball game, cheering for our team. Then we got back in the circle and walked around and around, until it got dark and cold, and then we straightened that circle into a line and we all walked home together.

My mother's main contribution to the protest, besides placards, enthusiasm, and her children, was a community poetry book. She wanted the university administrators, the other people on campus and in the city, even ourselves—a loose collection of broken families—to see us as a neighborhood, as a people worthy of saving. So first she held workshops in the community center. We did writing games and exercises, kids and adults together. Then we each picked our favorites to put into the book. We drew pictures, and those went in the book, too.

My mother was discovering poems: the writing of them, the publishing of them in small bound books, the reading of them in coffeehouses filled with smoke and bad lighting and sometimes a microphone, the power of them to fill up her empty spaces. The blank book in all its forms—lined, unlined, large, small, black or colored cover—was everywhere. Perhaps it was her helicopter. She joined poetry-writing groups, led workshops, taught poetry in the schools through special arts programs, and started making books, illustrating them with handmade prints, binding them with yarn and twine. Her passion was free speech and self-expression. She wanted children and adults to say what was on their minds, and she gave me my first blank book for my thirteenth birthday so I could say what was on mine.

My poem for the community anthology was called "Gatorville Sucks." It was all about the cockroaches and everything else I hated about our house, including the fact that it no longer housed my whole family. The picture accompanying my poem was of a cockroach, too—a long, thin matronly one ready to hatch a thousand babies that would then invade our beds and cupboards, crawling over our underwear and books and toothbrushes. My mother loved my poem for its feistiness and its veracity; even then I was bolder with the truth and with anger than she would ever be. Others in Gatorville, a neighborhood trying to present a united front against a pending eviction, did not love the poem and its many graphic depictions of everything bad about where we lived: the peeling paint; the pathetic swing set in the so-called playground; the front doors so easily broken into with just the swipe of a library card against the lock. My mother had to fight for it, but my poem and all its rage made it into the book. It was my shout against my circumstances—not just the roaches or the paint, but also against the divorce and the drugs, against the boys who groped me in closets and the men who rubbed their mounds on me on buses, against my father and older brother for leaving, and my mother for being so deluded by optimism that she sang loud happy songs in public, on the sidewalks and in school hallways, while I walked ahead, embarrassed and telling her to shut up, shut up.

But she was too wise, at that moment, to shut up. She didn't play her guitar anymore as she'd traded it in for a sewing machine so she could make quilts. (In a few years, she'd trade the sewing machine in for a juicer, then another sewing machine, then back to a guitar; she lived in a spiral of desires and tried to accommodate them all.)

But right then she was writing poems, putting her voice on paper in jagged rows.

Once, as an adult, I heard a young man interviewed on public radio. He stuttered, badly. His whole childhood he'd been beaten by his drunken stepfather in the trailer where they lived. Now he played on his high school basketball team in a small town in rural Pennsylvania. "I, I, I'm going to be the next Michael Jordan," he said over the airwaves, for everyone to hear. His voice was bloated, pumped up with the pathetic boastfulness of the destitute. That thought, that *dream*, is what confined the bruises and welts to the surface of the skin, rather than seeping inside to damage his internal organs. It's what he saw when the pain got so bad his eyes glazed over. His Michael Jordan dream—not just a basketball dream, not just an NBA dream, but a dream of colossal fame and excellence—is what kept him alive.

I, too, felt that I was one of the chosen few, destined for greatness. "Frances The Great," I painted in red on the sidewalk in front of our peeling-paint stairwell in Gatorville. No one ever told me this about myself; I believe I made it up out of nothing. I believe I made it up precisely because I had nothing.

At that point in my life, I knew how poor people dreamed. But as I got older, I began to wonder what dreams were like for the Haves of this world. Were they large and amorphous like mine, storm clouds all puffed up with the erratic power of thunder and lightning? Did their fantasies infuse them, like mine did, with the thrill of invincibility, with the kind of grandiosity that comes from booze or cocaine or excessive praise? Did the Haves know the excitement that sprints through the bloodstream, even as, tucked somewhere into those red cells, there is the understanding that this is a false rush, a delicious, exciting lie that will soon—oh, too soon!—evaporate, plucking you off the celestial and dropping you back to your small space on earth with a thud?

Or did the Haves dream more concretely? Perhaps their imaginations ran to solid constructions—to wood and steel, to architectural drawings in blue ink with block print showing exactly how to take this idea and plant it on the ground and build it into something real. Maybe they saw their future as clearly and inevitably as if it were a photograph of something taken before it's actually happened, rather than a wish that will never come true. Maybe this was how the rich differed from the rest of us—in the way that they dreamed. Perhaps it was as simple as the difference between *doing* and *thinking about doing*, between the vibrance of inhabiting your one and only life and the muted sense of waiting around for something to happen to you.

If so, then I yearned to see the world through their eyes, to assume without the slightest effort that I was worthy of whatever happened to delight or intrigue me, to be saturated so thoroughly with a belief in possibility that it wouldn't seem like a belief at all, but like a fact. Maybe it is vision that makes the rich different from you and me. Their eyesight is better; not more accurate, but definitely better. Dreaming or awake, they see the world

as if it were possible, which is certainly a more advanta-
geous way of viewing the world, as it allows you to actually make something of it.

People like me, on the other hand, have tantalizing
visions of the impossible, and often dream of fame and
celebrity. And my dream, once I got whisked away in the
helicopter, was the movies. This is not a very original
dream. People from my neighborhood often fantasized
of becoming movie stars or rock stars or athletic stars,
though my version was distinct. Because I had learned to
run the lights and the camera in fifth grade, had looked
through the little viewfinder that gave such blessed order
to the world, I wanted to *make* the movies, not appear in
them. But first I had to wait for that helicopter to call out
my name and whisk me away.

CHAPTER 7
MEET THE GIFTED CLASSES

It helps to be a girl and to be white. At school, for instance—an L-shaped junior high with four floors and an upper and lower yard covered in blacktop and painted with white and yellow lines—you get to mess up a few more times before getting sent to the dean or sent home or suspended or expelled altogether. In seventh grade, within a month of enrolling in my new school, I got into a fight with a boy, also white, also new to the school. I started the fight, just like I started fights with my brothers at home. For some reason the cool kids—the smokers, the stealers—who I was hanging around were picking on this guy and his twin sister, both quiet, pale, earnest. His locker was right below mine, giving me the opportunity to slam the metal door on his finger, on purpose. Immediately we assumed that classic school-fight choreography in the hallway: a ring of kids around us, him and me in the middle, stalking each other round and round, nudging shoulders, then throwing punches and rolling on the ground. Someone broke it up and we got sent to the dean's office. It was a fight between a boy and a girl. I was small. It was not hard to convince those in charge that he had started it.

During school, the worst thing that could happen was to get sent to Mr. Evans, the boys' dean. He was tall, built, a very dark black man who dressed sharp and wore his afro cropped close to his head. The rumor was he had a white wife. There were probably laws, by that time, against teachers hitting students, but Mr. Evans was above the law. I was lucky to be a girl and to get sent to the old white lady girls' dean instead.

But *afterschool*—a time and a place suspended—the white advantage wore off. Afterschool was open season. If you looked at somebody wrong or were friends with someone who did, they'd catch up with you afterschool. It was often black against white, and you got a warning. The word came down at recess or in the hallway that you'd better watch out afterschool. Then you had to decide: Should you sail right into it, act like you had done nothing wrong, had no one to fear, and either bluff or convince them out of it? Or just let them take you, an unresponsive target that would prove so unsatisfying they'd give up before they hardly started. Or you could try to avoid them, take a back way home to Gatorville, skip the bus stop and streetcar altogether and walk down side streets, hoping they didn't get so frustrated that they hunted you down.

For a while, the vice principal stationed himself at the streetcar stop two blocks away from the school. He was a big guy, Italian, in a gray suit. I once heard a colleague greet him by his first name, and as a joke I started calling him "Al" as well. I was just cute and white and small and female enough to get away with it, though his smile had a fair amount of grimace in it when I said his name. Al would not hesitate to reach in and break up a fight on the little cement island where we stood afterschool, waiting for the streetcar. But mostly he prevented fights from even starting just by standing there in his size and his suit. When he sent other teachers down to take his place at the corner, they were not so effective. Some wimpy white teacher in a skirt—she had no sway over a group of kids who, even if they were only twelve or thirteen, wanted to start something.

Stores were another place where it helped to be white. The salesclerks would watch the black girls while I glided around under the radar, slipping things into my pockets: lip gloss, earrings, a little folding hairbrush that flipped open like a switchblade. It was like being in a play. I had to convince myself that the stuff was rightfully mine, that it ended up in my book bag because I'd bought it. Then my body would act innocent all on its own; it would not cower in front of the shopkeepers or the other customers.

How do you make your body tell a lie? You have to make it believe it's telling the truth. It's all in how you walk and stand, how you move your head and hands and especially your eyes—which should never dart around but should instead scan for people in a slow, casual meander, while pretending that you are scanning for merchandise, looking for some item in particular. Also, stay visible; don't try to slip by undetected and don't hide out in back by the overstuffed sale racks. The best thing to do is to go right up to the salesclerk and ask a question, like, "Excuse me, where are the dress pants?" Be polite, demure, and don't wear make-up or high-heeled shoes. Look as white and innocent and legitimate as can be, as if your mother had just given you a twenty dollar bill and sent you to buy a new pair of school pants. After you have shoved the jeans into your book bag, your heart will be throbbing and your instinct will be to shoot out the door. But you must saunter instead. Speed is a give away; linger in front of the blouses on display, maybe ask another question or thank the clerk for her help. Walk out the door with the nonchalance of those unimpressed cockroaches who lived in your flat, as if you could buy or not buy anything you wanted. Then snag a shopping cart and glide down the hill toward home.

In the second semester of seventh grade, I got transferred into what was then called the "gifted" classes. It was there that I got to know real people, not just ones on TV, who were gifted in every sense of the word—gifted with homes and meals and stereos and cars and vacations and gifted also with a faith in the world and their place in it that was, and still is, foreign to me. Until that semester, the world was full of kids like me, kids whose parents were struggling to keep them fed, clothed, in school, and out of trouble. Kids who'd arrived accidentally and too soon, who spent a lot of time on their own, scheming and scamming, like their parents, to get by. Kids who zipped up their blue-hooded sweatshirts on a damp Saturday morning and stuffed the rest of their clothes in a pillow case, then lugged it down the street to the Laundromat

and dumped it and a couple quarters into the machine.
Kids who made their own lunches and got sent to Safe-
way with booklets of orange-and-white food stamps to
buy milk or tuna fish or a quarter-pound of bologna
from the meat counter, and kept their fingers crossed that
the cashier would have a heart and give them real change
back instead of the coupons for 58 or 35 or 22 cents.

Then suddenly I was plopped into the middle of these
school classes filled with the middle classes, kids, mostly
white, many Jewish, wearing braces, getting driven to and
from school by their parents, bringing homemade lunches
in crisp white paper bags, bags not oversized and brown
and wrinkled from carrying home a half-gallon of milk
and a loaf of bread, but bought in a package expressly for
the purpose of packing school lunches. Every morning
they picked these bags, plump with promise, off clean tile
counters. Then at lunch period, they brought them outside to the benches in the yard, rather than inside the cafeteria where the rest of us were eating hot lunch for free
or reduced price, our parents having filled out the forms,
putting the right numbers into the right columns. They
ate outside, with the clean smell of fog and eucalyptus,
and got first dibs on the handball court, and left portions
of their lunches—half a sandwich, a baggie of raisins—to
the seagulls who flew up from Ocean Beach and hovered
above the schoolyard waiting until the bell rang and we
ran in for class.

The first lesson of the Gifted Program was that
money makes you smart. Poor kids go to the regular and
dumb classes; rich kids go to gifted. I'm not sure how

I got to cross the line; some teachers must have "identified" me, as my parents would never have requested
such a thing. There also appeared to be some connection
between color and smarts, but I was white and so I could
pass, could slip by and seem to fit in with the gifteds even
if I didn't. The San Francisco Unified School District
used to send its notices home in English, Spanish, Chinese, and Tagalog, so the color line was far from black and
white. But it was there nonetheless. I had a social studies
teacher—she was also coach of the public speaking club I
had joined—who once told me about how she wouldn't
let a black girl in her class go to the "baffroom" until she
could say it properly. She told me this as a joke between
two people of the same color and, she assumed, class. But
all I could feel was the pressure of a full bladder and the
fear of peeing in front of thirty kids as a teacher taunts me
over something I don't understand.

What happens to a poor white girl who gets trans-
planted into the gifted classes? A girl with a way of thinking based equally on logic and emotion, whose affinity
for schoolwork, like her younger brother's affinity for
sports, could be traced in part to the void left by the
recent divorce which split not only the parents but also
the three children from each other? At first I wonder if
a mistake has been made. My confidence, the sassy way
I hold my own against my brothers and the other boys
in the neighborhood, leaks out of me like water from the
bottom of a potted plant. In class, I don't raise my hand
or join the discussion. I'm not even sure what the others are talking about—is it possible they are speaking in

a different language? Like an exile from another country, I don't know where to sit at lunch time, don't know what to do when my old friends—the ones I used to cut school with, to go smoking in the bushes or stealing lip gloss from Woolworth's—call me "traitor" as we pass in the hallway.

Eventually, my curiosity, my creativity, and my yearning for praise take over. One day in English when I am left standing with just one other student in the spelling contest, it dawns on me that I am as smart as these gifted kids. One of those kids, an especially kind Jewish girl with honey-blonde hair and perfect manners, lives on the way to my house, and we start to walk home together, and pretty soon she invites me over. We walk into the kitchen and drop our backpacks onto the counter next to the stacks of towels that have been washed, dried, and folded by the cleaning lady, and my friend opens a huge refrigerator filled to bursting. Like in a filmstrip, her voice narrates the scene inside the fridge: "We could have salami and crackers, grilled cheese with pickles, turkey and mustard…" Then she opens the freezer—it runs the whole length of the fridge—and continues the narration, "Orangesickles, mini pizzas, frozen Milky Way bars…" as frost pours into the kitchen like the five o'clock fog coming off the bay.

After our snack, we go up a carpeted staircase to her bedroom. Though she has her own desk and chair, she prefers to do homework on the thick fluff of her peach-colored carpet, and, therefore, so do I. The bedroom has two doors, one that leads to the landing, and one that leads to a bathroom with clean white tiles and a fuzzy blue rug on the floor and a matching fuzzy blue cover on the toilet seat (a cover for a toilet seat!). On the other side of this bathroom is another door, leading to her brother's room. The parents have their own bathroom in their bedroom. And there is yet another bathroom downstairs, in a little room near the kitchen. After homework, we put our books and binders away and listen to Elton John sing "Goodbye, Yellow Brick Road" on her very own stereo. Then we go down to the game room in the basement, where we play ping pong and, one time, where I eat dog food on a dare. As the hour turns from 3:30 to 4:30 to 5:30, and the sky goes from hazy blue and white to dark purple, the smells of cooking start to wind their way from the kitchen down to the game room. Some evenings, my friend conferences discreetly with her mother—who initiates these talks, I wonder, does the daughter ask the mother or does the mother ask the daughter?—and I get invited to dinner, a meal in which a half a pink grapefruit or an artichoke waits in its own little bowl at each setting, and cloth napkins sit in wooden holders brought back from the safari in Africa, and the father and mother and sister and brother take their seats and slip those napkins out of their holders and onto their laps, then slowly, punctuated by the foreign language of polite conversation, work their way through the first course, the main course, and dessert.

"Don't you need to call home," the mother asks, her teeth as big and white as the pearls in her ears, "to let your parents know where you are?" That's when a queasy panic seeps into my gut. How much should I tell? First, there's no parents, there's just a mom. Second, Mom's not home—she's either at class or at work. Also, there's no dinner waiting on the table. There's fish sticks in the freezer, or ground beef in the fridge, which my younger brother and I can shape into patties, put in the frying pan, then flip and press down on with a spatula, sending the juice, red and clear, sizzling into the grease, and then top with a couple slices of bright orange cheddar cheese, covering the pan to help the cheese melt, and filling all four rooms of the house with the smell of frying meat.

"Oh, no," I say. "It's fine. My mom won't mind." Sometimes, to make things go more smoothly, I accept the offer to use the phone, and I pretend to call my number, and, speaking to the dial tone in the refined way in which my friend speaks to her mother, I ask for permission to stay for dinner. And if it is winter, which in San Francisco doesn't mean snow but rain and wind and early darkness, the mother again conferences, this time with the father, a man in a suit whose first name is never told to me so I don't know how to address him, and it will be decided that the father will drive me home, and the only thing left to decide is if the daughter will accompany us in the car. The panic now gushes inside me, because even though it's cold and dark and possibly raining, even though the walk is almost forty-five minutes long, I must prevent the father—or at all costs the daughter—from seeing where I live: a clump of old army barracks with gray asphalt siding and peeling-paint porches, a place that looks no better in darkness than in light.

The dreary truth of the place I called home was just one of the things I didn't want the gifted kids and their families to know about me. I also worried, for instance, that they might discover that I stole my beautiful royal-blue, brush-denim jeans from the Emporium, stuffed them into a shopping bag after first stopping at another shop in the mall looking innocent and studious, with my schoolbooks about to fall unless the salesclerk would be so kind as to give me a shopping bag, new, unwrinkled, and imprinted with the store's logo so it worked like a hall pass that read "I'm a shopper—not just a looker, and certainly not a shoplifter," and then walking confidently into the next store, where I shoved my new wardrobe under the books in the shopping bag so I could look sort of like the gifted kids. What if the kids at school realize that my running shoes are a cheap plastic no-name imitation of the real thing? What if they find out that my parents are divorced, my mother doesn't have a car, and my dad drives a dirty old International pick-up that he works on himself? What if they find out that we don't have a lawn or a dishwasher? Or that I'm not really Jewish, despite my last name, and have never been to a seder or a temple, know nothing about Zionism or keeping kosher? What if they learn that I've never stayed in a motel or traveled to a foreign country? That I've done drugs, cut school, stayed out late without my parents knowing or caring? That I've lied, stolen, and started fights? That I get no allowance, qualify for free lunch in the cafeteria, and walk home in order to save the five-cent bus fare? But most of all, I worried about them finding out where I lived.

—

Of course they had to find out eventually. On my thirteenth birthday, I went home sick to this crescent of army barracks. I'd been in bed with a fever for several days but had forced myself to go into school so I could be around people on the one day of the year when I could hope to get a fuss made over me. But it was a mistake to go in; I was weak and had to leave early, sweating on the streetcar, then shivering as I walked down the foggy hill. My friends at school had been surprised to see me that morning in the yard waiting for the bell, and they were oddly pleased to see me go before lunch period. But I was too hot and cloudy-headed to think much about how they acted and why.

Then, at around 3:30 in the afternoon, reading in the bed that I shared with my mother, I heard the sleigh bells of girl voices, faint, then closer and closer. An image so horrifying that I had never even imagined it was materializing outside the window: six or seven of the gifted girls were walking down my street, toward my door, carrying a white bakery box and bright armfuls of packages along with their book bags. I had sixty, maybe ninety seconds to get the house clean and somewhat respectable before they figured out which door was mine, and I ran around turning on lights, making beds, swatting the crumbs off the sheet that covered the foam mattress that sat on the floor of the front room posing as a couch.

The rest of the afternoon I remember only in flashes, like the dreams that come with delirium: their happy colors in my gray doorway; not enough forks or chairs; the girls wondering where my mother was, since I was home, sick; and how quiet it all seemed when they finally left and I was alone again, surrounded by the bright shreds of ribbon and wrapping paper, feeling a red nakedness burning like the fever inside me and wondering how I could ever show my face at school again.

It took me a few days to recover from the birthday party and the flu, but I finally went back to school. These girls were brought up well. They already knew how to ignore uncomfortable facts and smile with extreme kindness and many straight, white teeth, to ask after your health and make sure you were invited to almost all the get-togethers. They acted as if nothing had changed, and I tried to follow their lead. But their graciousness did little to mitigate my shame. They were a part of a group of girls that liked to pass around things for you to sign and hand off to the next kid—notes written on binder paper, yearbooks, "slam books" with questions on your favorite bands, TV shows, and which boy you'd like to slow dance with. At the end of eighth grade, even though we didn't graduate for another year, I was collecting autographs in my own little book. "Dear Frances," wrote one girl, per-haps the first girl I ever hated, "I'm so glad you became part of The Group this year."

They think they're doing you a favor by letting you in, moving you up, buying your ticket for you. But to be *let in* is the start of a hidden life with knowing looks and gracious smiles and wondering who's heard the truth. It is the start of shame—not the shame of doing something mean, like keeping a girl out of the hopscotch game, but the shame of simply being the only person you are. In my case, it was also the start of a bifurcation, splitting me into two worlds, and a philosophy, which I came to call the "exclusion principle," that allowed me to navigate between those worlds. Here's how it worked: When the teacher passed out the notices about the yearbook going on sale, or a blood drive or a PTA fundraiser, I took those pale pink or green sheets of paper like everyone else, pretending I would deliver them to my parents. Then, when no one was looking, I crumpled them up and threw them away. Those things were for other people to participate in, but not for me. My folks didn't have the money or the time or the urge, and I didn't want to add to their burden. So I excluded myself from whatever opportunity or obligation was being offered to everyone else.

By day, I went to school, trying to pass as gifted. By night, the shame turned into anger at my mother for singing, at my father for sulking, at my little bedroom with a curtain for a door, at my brothers and the kids in the neighborhood and the scrappy clothes that we all wore. It turned into anger at men and boys and dreams and at whatever it was that made things unfair, that created the Haves and the Have Nots and put me on the wrong side. At home I was a fury, yelling at my mother about everything we didn't have, and all that I thought she was doing wrong: carrying a backpack instead of a purse like the other moms did; telling us outlandish stories, like one about riding on the bus driver's lap, that were hard to believe but even harder not to believe; flitting from one pursuit to the next, from poetry to Japanese brush painting to quilting to dance to knitting and back to poetry again. She tended to deflect my criticism with a large smile and a rhetorical question: "There's something wrong with my backpack?" But if I really wanted to get to her, I could call her "crazy," like my dad used to do. Then her eyes flashed, her smile fell, and she'd walk away or get fierce right back at me.

Meanwhile, the university was sending out negotiators to meet with the Gatorville residents who were heading up the protest against tearing down our crummy houses and replacing them with a parking lot. The college's offer—and it was tantalizing—was to put us up for the duration of our leases in a private housing development on the other side of the campus. These were not the projects; these were real private homes, with a generic suburban tidiness that seemed opulent to us. But the deal was they would only be ours for a year at our current rental rates. After our leases ran out, we'd have to pay the market value—three or four times what we were paying for the university housing—or, more likely, be out on the streets looking for another cheap place to live much farther from campus. One afternoon we met the university man at of one of these houses, a two-story duplex bordered with lawn and hedges, so he could give us a closer look. We knew the offer was really a bribe, since it required us to stop the protest and pull out of the legal battle in exchange for a limited time in a house like this. And we knew that we had the moral, as well as the practical, obligation to turn down the offer, because the fight wasn't just for us, the current residents, but also for students in the future who would need an affordable place to house themselves and their families while they all went to school. Still, it was hard to walk around those soundless carpeted floors, to run our fingers along the formica in the kitchen, to look at the staircase that divided the bedrooms from the living rooms, without drooling.

The university man wore a suit and an over-trying smile. It was an outfit I had seen before on the real estate salesmen we met when my dad had tried to move us to the country. He led a half-dozen harried parents and a dozen rowdy kids from room to room. The parents walked slowly, trying to muffle their desire, while the kids ran up and down the stairs, opening and closing windows and doors, shouting out about the icemaker in the fridge and the light *inside* the oven and how there was a bathroom on each floor and each bedroom had its own closet, and asking, "Are we going to live here, Mom? Is this our new house?" The university man winced against the noise, but he knew it was helping his cause, and so he worked even harder on his smile. Then he caught sight of me, a twelve- or thirteen-year-old girl, who was standing with the pack of adults. Even then I knew this house was a tease, that we would move, and then move again and again, but we would never live in a place like this, a place I could invite anyone into. The university man widened his eyes, as if asking me how I liked the place, as if the decision were mine to make. I met his gaze and just shook my head no.

Years later I would return to see what had happened to our neighborhood, finally ready to take a look at the parking lot that had replaced our homes. I took the streetcar and then walked down the sloping hill toward the basin. When I reached the ledge where the shortcut had been, and looked down to see the inevitable, I was hit with a shock that no one could have prepared me for. Instead of asphalt and metal, instead of white lines and rows of cars, there was a massive, gleaming lawn. We had believed that concrete was the enemy, but grass, it turns out, is meaner than you'd think. A bright happy green was growing over everything, over the streets and the speed bumps where we used to pop wheelies on our bikes, over the laundry room and the free box where we'd played whippersnappers, over the community center and the giant eucalyptus trees that draped over it, over the catwalks and staircases and bedrooms, wiping out every last vestige of our lives, even the cockroaches.

Down on the lawn where our houses and streets used to be, a young man, who probably lived in the dorms nearby, was practicing his punts with a football. He'd kick the ball, then jog down the field to retrieve it before kicking it back the other way. I had the urge to shout out to him, "Don't you do that," as if he were playing in a church. But instead I walked the long way down to the access road, the one street that still remained, and then walked along the sidewalk to the spot where my building had stood. There, painted on the curb, were our names: Caleb L.; Juan + Delmar rule; Frances the Great. I don't know how they'd survived.

CHAPTER 8
SWITCH ROLES WITH YOUR MOTHER

After the eviction from the university housing, my mother, my younger brother, and I moved to a greenhouse. Actually, it was a house with a glass greenhouse attached to it, which, my mother explained with bright enthusiasm, would serve as a bedroom for one of us. The flat, in the avenues near Golden Gate Park, was in a one-family home that had been divided into two flats. The owners were on sabbatical and agreed to sublet us their garden apartment for the year, even agreeing to the bureaucratic demands of the Section 8 federal housing assistance program my mother had recently been granted, along with food stamps and MediCal (which allowed us to go to the doctor with a dollar and a sticker from the blue-and-white sheet sent to us monthly). The flat had a backyard with a plum tree, and was located within walking distance of the arboretum in the park, a place with delightful winding paths, a patch of manicured wildness in the city, where I would spend many afternoons studying and daydreaming, often about the boys from my junior high who I wished would take me walking or skateboarding down those paths, hand in hand. The only problem with the flat—aside from the fact that we'd have to leave it after a year—was the bedroom situation. It had one official bedroom, plus a front room converted to a bedroom, plus that homemade greenhouse at the back of the house that would, as my mother vowed, be a great bedroom for somebody.

Indeed, that glassed-in room flanked by the deep purple leaves of the plum tree struck both my brother and me as idyllic, and we fought over which of us would get to claim it as our own. Though he was beginning to grow into his full size, he was still my little brother, ten years old to my thirteen, and no match for my nasty determination. I'd lived in that closet in Gatorville, after all, and there was no way this glorious room, with its view of the garden and its promise of sun, was going to go to someone other than me. My mother had no part in the decision-making; even if she had tried to step in and arbitrate, she had already abdicated this kind of parental control, as had my father. Instead, my brother and I used these methods to resolve the conflict: yelling, cajoling, arguing, bribing, commiserating, kicking, scratching, leaning, pinching, sweet-talking, threatening, and insulting. In the end, I won, and this victory, I believe, cemented a rift between my brother and me that would take years to get over. It wasn't fair, and we both knew it, but there were only two people in the world that I had any power over—my mother and this brother—and I used it here.

A couple months after we moved in, the rains, and the leaks, began. Nearly every seam of caulking holding every piece of glass in my greenhouse bedroom was faulty. For a while, I placed buckets and bowls, coffee cans and cottage-cheese containers under the drips, but there was no catching this water. Like the cockroaches in my old Gatorville bedroom, the rain claimed this room as its own, ignoring and even laughing at my attempts to stop it. With the water came the cold and also the mold, which ruined homework and fouled my clothes. Once again, I ended up in my mother's bed in the converted living room that was her bedroom.

While my brother was off making friends with whatever males were available—the bachelor upstairs, the guy who ran the ice cream shop up the street—my mother was breaking through three more barriers no one ever imagined she'd cross: she got a driver's license, a car, and a boyfriend. The car was an unreliable, faded red VW squareback that broke down when she took it on a trip to Yosemite—another thing she'd never been expected to do. It lasted for a year or two before she had to get rid of it, but still, her accomplishment was unmistakable, and she glistened with pride.

As for the boyfriend, a kind, willowy, soft-spoken blond man from New Orleans who studied poetry at State with my mother, I took it upon myself to get rid of him. It was a mild, blue-sky Thanksgiving Day when he arrived at our door with a bottle of red wine. We had carried the table out of the kitchen and set it up in the entryway, which we were pretending was our dining room. My mother had been buzzing around like a hummingbird all morning, and I'd followed her lead, trying to make our stuff—worn red tablecloth, mismatched chairs—look better than it actually was. She basted the turkey and I spread cream cheese on celery, sprinkled it with paprika and arranged it on a plate in a circle. She put chrysanthemums in a vase on the table, and I folded the napkins into triangles and put them at each place setting. Underneath the excitement was a current of anxiety: my mother's from hoping everything would turn out all right between her guest and her kids, and mine from wishing none of this was happening at all, that we were just back at our old flat on 16th and Sanchez with my dad, the way it used to be. My brothers—my older brother had taken the bus over from where he lived with my dad—were on their bellies in the corner of the mock dining room, watching football on TV and munching on those cream-cheese celery sticks. Unfortunately for us all, I was not as good as they were at watching TV or ignoring tension.

When the wispy blond man came in the door, my mother kissed him and then introduced him to her children: two nonchalant boys, ten and fifteen, barely looking up from the television, and one suspicious thirteen-year-old girl wondering suddenly if this man was where all her mother's energy was flowing these days, if he was the reason she was so rarely home. Suddenly, all that effort my mom and I had put toward making things nice felt like not only a lie but also a cheat. We hardly even ate dinner together anymore—my mother was rushing around between jobs and classes—but for this man, my mother had cooked up a feast.

My mother went off to the kitchen with the man and

his wine. My brothers returned their gaze to the game. I stood in the doorway. A churning in the pit of my stomach that started out as nausea and morphed quickly into wrath took over my chest, shoulders, and forearms, which were arrow-straight ending in tight fists. I had no choice but to make everyone else miserable, too. First I stomped over to my brothers and snatched up the tray of celery.

"Save some for the rest of us," I snarled. Then I brought the tray into the kitchen and shoved it toward the guest. "Have some," I told him.

He smiled, hesitant.

"Go on. It's my mom's specialty. Except it was me who made it. She doesn't actually make much food anymore."

"Frances!" my mom said, in a playful tone that she hoped would run me off track. But I was already committed, my wheels locked in.

"Unless she cooks for *you*," I said, still facing the guest, daring him to take a piece of celery.

But he was too easy a target, as deferential as a leaf, and not really the object of my rage. That was my mother; she was the one, after all, who had filed the paperwork which divorced my family from itself, and was now trying desperately to mother herself along with her children. My father deserved to share in my wrath, but he protected himself with a serene detachment that somehow gave off the impression that he had little to do with the way his children's lives were turning out. So I hid my emotions from him and lashed out at my mother and brothers instead. At the Thanksgiving dinner table, my mother smiled nervously and her shy friend tried to talk football with my brothers, though he was really more interested in poetry. But I could not let this peace prevail. All was not right with our family, and I couldn't pretend that things were fine, even just for one day. I don't remember what exactly I harped on, but I provoked until my mother responded, "That's not a nice thing to say," and then I provoked some more. My brothers tried calming me down with mild, soothing insults, but I yapped at them, too. By the end of the meal, I was on my back on the floor, in the kind of full-blown crying-yelling fit that you'd only expect to see in a two-year-old, if that two-year-old had phrases such as "fuck you, you mother-fucking asshole bitch" in her vocabulary. The soft blond man finally had the wherewithal—and instinct for self-preservation—to realize he'd stumbled upon an impossible situation, and excused himself. My brothers also left, to toss the football in the street. My mother didn't know whether to cry or yell, so she just clammed up, refusing to look at me. She cleared the table, put the food away, and I slinked off to my leaky glass-walled greenhouse, alone.

My embarrassment was only matched by my guilt at ruining the holiday, as well as my mom's relationship with a man whose only fault was that he was not my father. If my mother ever dated again, she wisely kept it a secret from me. But on several occasions she told me, "If I had a man's love, then I could love you better." Which only made me ever more suspicious of this kind of love—a man's—that was keeping me from getting what I wanted.

—

When our year was up, we had to find another place that would take on Section 8 renters. The place Mom found was located on a sooty bus route on 14th Street, just up from the busy artery of Market Street, a long streetcar ride away from my high school and her college. It had a double front room separated by sliding wooden doors, which we kept closed so one side became my brother's room, the other served as a combination living room and bedroom for my mother. My room was at the end of the narrow hallway on the other side of the kitchen. The bonus room was a large walk-in closet—reminiscent of the one that had served as my bedroom in Gatorville—which served as my mother's office and, during one phase when she sought privacy, her bedroom as well.

We had now moved eight times since I was born, all within the confines of the city, except for that brief attempt to find Land in Clear Lake. But this was the first time we were living in an area that wasn't really a neighborhood, just a place where people stayed for a while before moving on to someplace better or someplace worse. The foot traffic and the car traffic were both heavy, and the only people we knew by sight were the ones who lived on the sidewalk. A block away was a park famous for dog shit, and up the hill was a park famous for the men who fucked each other in the bushes. On the other side of dog-shit park were the bus stops and butcher shops and liquor stores that served the housing projects of the Fillmore district, projects since razed and replaced with less affordable housing. Our triangle of streets, caught between the Castro, the Fillmore, and Market Street, was what developers called "in transition," bracing itself for gentrification. Nowadays, as with most of the areas where we used to live, it is filled with places to get sushi and cappuccino and handcrafted doorknobs for kitchen cabinets, and those of us who used to live there couldn't afford it even if we wanted to.

Since the flat sat directly on the sidewalk, we could hear the conversations of everyone who walked by: gay guys screaming at each other, straight couples getting horny on each other, the bag lady with the rat teeth muttering and sometimes yelling to herself. Encased in metal bars, we could, at night, also see these amblers, their silhouettes trapped between the streetlights and the window shade, unaware, we hoped, that on the other side of that thin membrane of a wall we lay in our beds, trying to dream ourselves away.

City kids have a walk, limbs loose but controlled, a heavy downbeat with one leg while the other glides. It's more than a walk. It's an attitude, tough but casual, pushing fear away by daring harm to approach—*don't even think about messing with me.* That was my walk when I got off the streetcar and headed up to our new flat, fingering my key in my pocket. When I got to the black metal gate, I'd whip out the key, let myself in, and lock up, all in one smooth, quick second, in case anyone was trying to follow me in. Occasionally I'd get a ride home from school—several of my classmates were driving now and had cars—but I'd always get them to drop me off at a friend's house, or on the street corner, so they couldn't see

where I lived. I passed as normal at school, maybe even
confident, wearing protective layers of sarcasm along
with my jeans, cowboy boots, and vintage-style sweaters
I'd found at the thrift store. It was an image I did not want
to disturb, so I kept even my closest friends away from
my home.

Our new setting only seemed to enhance the arguments between my mother, myself, and my younger
brother, who felt it was especially unfair that he had to
live with us instead of the men in his family. He was right
in this, as he'd get nagged by my mother and then by me
as well since I didn't trust my mother to nag him properly. I didn't trust my mother to do anything properly,
especially things like feeding and sheltering and protecting. And so I did these things for myself, for my brother,
and bit by bit for my mother as well. As I discovered, a big
part of mothering is worrying. I worried about the Section 8 paperwork, about the new MediCal co-pay rules,
about the food stamps running out before the end of the
month, about how much one could earn at work before
the welfare department started deducting from your
check. And I worried about food.

People like us, poor, cynical, ambitious, we eat for
fullness more than for flavor. We are hungry for a sense
of sureness, and we eat to tether ourselves to the earth so
we don't float away like candy wrappers in the gutter. In
the apartment, at the end of the narrow hallway, the cupboards in our kitchen were almost bare, partly from a lack
of money and time, and partly because my mother was
becoming a calorie-conscious vegetarian who perpetually

believed, like so many women, that she should shed a few pounds, though she actually had very few to lose. We had a dinner table, but dinner was a distant memory, and I could no longer recall a time when the family of five, or even three, had sat around together tasting, chewing, swallowing, talking. There were ten years when we must have all eaten together, but I was—and still am—unable to conjure up a single image of my family around the dinner table, and I have no idea who sat where, what we ate, what we teased and laughed about.

I vaguely remember my father slicing carrots and scallions into thin slivers for ramen noodle soup at the too-expensive flat on Harrison Street that we moved into after we came back from Clear Lake. A couple times he brought crab home to this same apartment; from his wood shop on the piers, he'd toss a net over and sometimes pull up a few edible-sized crabs from the questionable waters of the bay. On 16th and Sanchez, I remember my mother boiling up beef tongue and corned beef with potatoes and carrots and cabbage, a spoonful of mustard on the side for dipping. She used to make a pineapple upside-down cake in a black skillet, and once, for my father's birthday, she baked a sponge cake into the shape of a giant cigarette, frosted white with a red-ember end. She had quit smoking and this was her way of trying to get him to quit, too.

At our new flat on 14th Street, my mother, who was running between college classes, dance classes, poetry readings, and various part-time jobs, rarely cooked. In the fridge, she kept nonfat milk and nonfat yogurt, along with a head of broccoli or lettuce and a big pale hunk of part-skimmed mozzarella, the cheese with the lowest fat content available at the time. Sometimes she boiled up a chicken with carrots, and once, for Christmas dinner, she served us kids tofu-stuffed green peppers, which we ate on the floor in the room that acted as both the living room and my mother's bedroom.

We seemed to yearn, especially, for carbohydrates. If there was a loaf of bread in the house, any one of us—my mother, my younger brother, or myself—could end up in the kitchen after the others had gone to bed, and finish it off, hand to mouth at a hurried pace, each bite promising to finally satiate us. After school, when no one was home, I sometimes mixed up a paste of flour and water—all I could find in the pantry—and ate it, raw, from a little wooden bowl in the narrow darkness of the kitchen.

One evening, when I was fifteen, my mother confided in me that she might be pregnant by Bob Dylan. Dylan was bigger than the Beatles in our family, bigger, of course, than God. Just the way he mumbled and wore his hair seemed to impress us all, how he refused to make himself understood or categorized. He had just performed several concerts downtown, part of the "Slow Train Coming" tour, in which he sang mostly about finding Christ, someone my mother knew from childhood and who, at this point in time, she seemed to want to find again, as well.

"Mom," I whined, stretching the syllables like any teenage girl might say out of frustrated embarrassment, as if, say, her mother had just called her by a pet name in front of her friends. But quickly I switched to another tactic: logic.

"You don't even know Bob Dylan," I said, trying to argue my mother out of this outlandish claim.

But Mom reached into her black nylon daypack, felt for her wallet, and pulled out three ticket stubs for consecutive nights of concerts at the Market Street theater a few weeks earlier.

"I met him after the show," she said with such severe melancholy that she couldn't be lying.

At fifteen, I was already too old for my years, weary of wondering and worrying about my mother, and perched on the serrated edge of too many questions about her. But I was still young enough to write to Dylan, in care of Capitol Records, inquiring as to whether he had gone out with my mother during his recent performances in San Francisco. Dylan did not write back, and my mother, whose stomach never began to swell, told me a few weeks later that she had been speaking in metaphor, that she had told me that story so I could learn the difference between her lying and her telling the truth. By now I was bewildered, not sure what to believe.

Soon afterwards, three things happened: the landlord phoned to say that a plumber was coming to do some work on the building; our next-door neighbors told us to be wary of goings-on in the alley behind our house, as they had discovered a hole cut through their fence; and, in one of my mother's classes at the university, there was a discussion about an item in the gossip section of the local paper which reported that Bob Dylan had just spent twenty-five thousand dollars on a wedding ring.

My mother, who was writing a play about Emily Dickinson for her Master's thesis in creative writing, was able to make a kind of story out of these three things. According to her, the landlord had the neighbor contact us in order to see if my mother would be home so he could come visit her; the professor in her class had been sitting behind her at the Dylan concert and brought up the wedding-ring gossip as a way to tease my mother about her relationship with the rock star; and the plumber, when he came in the morning, would turn out *to be Bob Dylan himself*!

When someone wavers between creativity and eccentricity, between irrational delusion and brilliant resourcefulness, between poverty, despondency, and bright, genuine joy, it is hard to figure out what, as the helping professionals would later ask of me, seems to be the problem. Perhaps my mother *had* merely been speaking in metaphor, referring to the similarities between my dad—a man who *did* father children with her—and Dylan: both were young, audacious Jewish men with wild dark curls riding motorcycles into California just as the tide was turning from beatnik to hippie and from folk to rock. Perhaps my mother, a poet by nature, was simply reacting to the circumstances of her life, acting out a form of logic that made sense, given the dearth of love and money and other resources that had been spent on her. Or maybe she had a condition, a disorder, an abnormal way of seeing and feeling and being. Over and over and around and around for decades I would wonder if my mother's behavior was the sign of artistry or sickness or deep, deep honesty. Was it the necessary residue from a childhood of mistreatment by her mother, the nervous combustion between a vibrant and sensitive girl and the "no, no, no" she heard all around her in the Catholic schools and homes of the 1950s? Was she fragile or depressed, lonely or wise or unlucky? Or was she simply born with a larger heart and thinner skin and more sensory receptors and a bigger vocabulary and larger peripheral vision than the average person?

My mother had a genius for survival, and she managed especially well at just above the breaking point. She seemed almost to thrive on Empty, and was at her most ingenious hovering close to the edge, just getting the bills in on time, and living off pink grapefruits and black coffee sometimes watered down with nonfat milk. She always knew how to get herself into a jam so she could pull herself out at the last second, triumphant. But she also knew how to get flowers in a vase on the back of the toilet no matter how much cash she didn't have and to tell us shivering kids to do jumping jacks—that's what the children in Sweden do, she'd say, and it gets *really* cold there—when we were waiting at the bus stop on a damp, windy night. She knew how to find free or almost free classes for herself and her children—dance and drama for her and me, magic and photography for my brothers. And how to buy the tree for half-price on Christmas Eve and talk the streetcar driver into letting us carry it on, or, one year, to make her own tree out of a sheet of purple butcher paper cut into arched branches and taped onto the wall. And to ask "Poor in what? In money?" when, as a teenager in that iron-barred flat on 14th Street, I complained about all the things we did not have.

Years later I would come to see her as brave, resilient, and enterprising. But at the time—I was fourteen, fifteen, sixteen—all I knew was that things were shifting under my feet and neither wood nor linoleum nor sidewalk nor soil could be counted on to sustain me. For people on welfare, food stamps, and Section 8 housing subsidies, social workers or other representatives of the so-called helping professions are the same as cops: you try to avoid them and then, if they do come around, to appear as normal and clean as possible. There were always stories of kids being taken away from mothers who were deemed crazy, abusive, or filthy housekeepers. So I tended to keep my confusion and apprehension to myself, except when I was expelling it in loud rages against my mother over minor offenses. Perhaps the other members of my spread-out family were as upset as I was, but I seemed to be the one designated to act out all that frustration in fierce temper tantrums that would have shamed even a two-year-old.

One afternoon on the streetcar, around the time of the Dylan concerts, I ran into my dance teacher, a light-skinned black woman with freckles and high cheekbones. She was headed to the city rec center where she taught free ballet and jazz dance classes to children and adults, to my mother and to me.

"How is your mother?" she asked. The intonation was kind, delicate, concerned.

"She's fine," I said, automatically. Then I looked into her face. This was a street-smart single mother who could sense when things were off, who knew that a fifteen-year-old girl could sense this as well, but who also understood the dangers of disrupting the starfish-on-a-rock pull between mother and daughter. This was not a teacher at school or a social worker who could get my mother in trouble. This was not a friend who could shun me if she knew how I really lived.

"Sometimes," I said in a low voice, "I do worry about her."

We talked for a few minutes, quietly, vaguely.

"Do you have people you can talk to?" she asked.

"Oh, yeah," I said, not meeting her eyes.

Just before the tunnel that cut through a hill too steep for the streetcar to climb, her stop came up and she touched my shoulder, then stepped out the door. Her long hair was, as always, braided and wrapped around her head ballet-style, and her shoulder bag, stuffed with leotards and tights and little leather slippers in pink and black and white, bounced off her hip as she started up the hill. The streetcar entered the tunnel, revealing darkness, and then my reflection in the window, tinged with equal parts guilt and relief.

That night at home, my mom greeted me with a glare, holding back her words. I headed for my room, to the comforting respite of homework: chapters to read, facts to memorize, assignments to follow word by word.

"It's not polite to talk about people," my mother said. "Especially in public."

I stopped in the doorway. Did she know about the streetcar conversation, or was she omniscient? Was she a good guesser, or had she been sitting on a seat in the rear of the car that day, watching and hearing the whole delicate unburdening? Or perhaps she just happened to decide that today was the day to give me a little motherly lesson on good behavior.

"So please don't discuss me with anyone," she added.

I'm not sure of my response on this day, if I argued or acquiesced. Traditionally these interactions would turn me into a foot-stomping, door-slamming tyrant, screaming out all the things that proved my mother was crazy and stupid and mean, and yelling about how I couldn't wait to get out of high school and out of the house, and out of this life she'd given me and into a better one. But this may have been one of those rare times when I backed down, scared quiet by the searing look in her eyes and the pain smoldering just under the surface of her skin.

Our parents cannot provide us with everything we need, but with luck, other people, even strangers, may step in from time to time to fill a gap. When people came to me like this, they recognized the weight I carried on my small frame, and recognized also the lightness hidden underneath; they saw the fragility under the fierceness; they saw my youth. I'd been to summer camp on scholarship every year since I was eight, and one of my saviors was a counselor who noticed that I was not like the other kids learning to water ski and ride horses and stand at the archery range with one straight arm and one bent, feet wide, breath even, pulling the arrow back and letting it go. He was my friend for years, helping me to celebrate birthdays and graduations, including me on outings with his girlfriends, without ever making me feel like a charity case. He was the one who made a fuss over my sixteenth birthday, creating a slight commotion among my friends at school by picking me up in his VW van, treating me to my first line of cocaine—a right of passage in San Francisco in the late 1970s—and then to dinner at a restaurant named after my zodiac sign. This man also once gave me a one hundred dollar bill for Christmas, telling me I was not allowed to spend it on groceries.

And then there were the strangers. Once, when I was a junior in high school, I sat on the sidewalk on a notorious corner, leaning up against the Fillmore projects, waiting for a bus. It was midnight, and I should not have been there, but I was trying to get to a party—fun was happening somewhere and I wanted in. Three black guys crossed the street below, then sauntered up the hill casual-like, but aimed directly toward me. My head and stomach filled with dread, and the thought flashed across my mind that my fortune had finally run out, that after all my late-night bus riding and street walking without incident, I was due.

The weapon I had devised to protect myself on the streets was an attitude, not of toughness, but of a kind of confident insignificance. I was too petite to scare off anyone, so I always tried to appear even smaller, as if I had nothing—no money, no heft, no gender—and was therefore not worth bothering. I was busy conjuring up this attitude when the young men approached and stopped right in front of me. One leaned down to put his face into mine.

"What are you doing out here this time of night all by

yourself?" he said. "Somebody might do something bad to you." And just to make sure nobody did, he and his friends stayed with me till my bus came.

Another time, on a bright Saturday morning, I got up early for a school speech tournament, packed myself a lunch and a thermos of tea, and got dressed in the pink and brown cotton skirt, white ballet tights, and pink sweater that I thought gave me the right look of innocence and earnestness to sway the judges. The tournament was being held at a Catholic boys' school not too far from my own school, and our speech and debate team was gathering at the boys' school early for last-minute instructions. As I was rushing down my block to the streetcar stop, practicing my speech in my head, a man turned the corner and then stepped back to avoid a collision. He was lean and bearded, not too old, slightly disheveled and possibly, though not necessarily, homeless. Despite my run-ins with men, I had no apprehension about this one. He was harmless, amusing, even a bit sweet.

"Whoopsie," I said.

"No problem," he said.

I crossed onto the concrete island where the streetcar would be stopping, I hoped, any minute now. The man stood still, watching me as I fiddled around in my day pack for my coin, and tried to find a shaft of sun to stand in. His gaze had no sex or aggression to it, just a kind of awe, and I didn't really mind him looking at me. Traffic was light this early in the morning, and the bus stop was empty. The man did not have to shout for his voice to reach me.

"I hope you realize how beautiful you are," he said.

Except for an involuntary smile, I had no answer for him, and he moved on.

At the end of the tournament that day, I placed but did not win. In the chaos of winners and losers mulling around the school lobby, a judge from one of my preliminary rounds, a man in loafers and a navy-blue suit jacket, approached me. He, too, had something to say about my appearance.

"Your shoes," he said, pointing to the pale brown clogs buckled onto my feet. They were my best shoes, my version of heels, an off-brand that I hoped passed for the good kind, and the only shoes I had that could go with a dress. "They're a bit casual for competition." Same for the skirt, and the tights, and the sweater, too.

"You think my shoes cost me my event?" I said, trying to keep the sass out of my voice. It was in my best interest to be deferential, but I was developing the skill of self-sabotage instead.

"I'm just trying to help you out," he said.

At home, where there were no benevolent strangers, I had begun to stay up later than my mother, though often I was awake against my will, having turned off the lights and put the books aside but unable to relax into sleep. I was at the age when even rich and happy mothers and daughters are engaged in constant canine-like battles of dominance and submission, fighting and playing, clawing and cuddling. Yes, I had begun to lose faith in everything she said or did. Yes, I had begun to get the groceries and do the laundry, to fill out the school paperwork. Yes, I was cooking for my brother and myself whenever the two

of us were home at the same time. But it was still unnerv-
ing to be awake while the others in the house slept. I was
not ready to be the sentinel while my mother and brother
lay face down in their beds, their muscles limp, their hair
splayed out over the sheets.

My mother was nearing the end of her optimism, her
exuberance propelling her and spiraling out at the same
time, like the tail-fire of a comet. She'd stay out late for
a class or a poetry reading, while my brother might be
at my father's or out with friends, maybe he had a game,
football or baseball—nobody was keeping tabs. Like my
father, my mother meant us no harm, was not withhold-
ing anything from us on purpose. She was simply trying as hard as she could to accomplish everything she
needed and wanted to do. For a brief shiny moment, she
had imagined that she could pursue her dreams of self-
expression, that she could find a home in poetry and art
and education. But now her dreams seemed more like
fantasies, and she didn't see how she could ever make a
living out of them. So once again she assumed the posture of striving, so much more familiar and comfortable
to her than that of achieving. She'd gone to high school
with a famous bohemian family from Big Sur, and one
of those boys had gone on to become a renowned artist.
She'd tell me this story with such awe in her voice that
it saddened me. It was as if she were settling for brushes
with other people's success rather than securing her own.
Like my father and his quest for Land on which to bring
up his children, she was giving up on her desires even as
she seemed to go after them.

So off I'd go to school, and then, when classes were over, to speech-team practice or a play rehearsal or a meeting for Model UN or student council. Some of my friends liked to complain about school, but I flourished under the regimen and the expectations, the praise and the acceptance, and stayed as long as possible at that large campus on the edge of the city. I traveled back and forth between the nerdy kids cramming in the halls, the cool kids smoking down in the "pit," and the in-between kids stationed on the back lawn midway between the hall and the pit. Then I'd take the streetcar to my housecleaning job or back to my empty home. Sometimes my dad would come by, honking twice rather than risk ringing our doorbell and seeing my mother, and then take me out for coffee with the drag queens at the Café Flor in the Castro or the artists at the Café Trieste in North Beach. But then I'd come home and steam up some broccoli for dinner, grate some pale, rubbery mozzarella on top, then put a plate over the bowl to encourage the cheese to melt. I'd pack myself a lunch for the next day: some of that same nonfat mozzarella with an apple, a carrot, a slice of bread if we had some. Then I'd spend hours memorizing Spanish vocabulary and verb conjugations, learning the presidents of the United States in order along with the hallmarks of each administration, and writing about theme and setting in Shakespeare and Steinbeck. My mind could memorize, it could categorize, it could analyze, and by doing these things it saved me from a desolation that I sensed was hovering like a vulture somewhere above me, waiting for weakness and inactivity.

But late at night, after tucking myself in, I couldn't fall asleep until my mother came home. For all my attitude and fortitude, for all her weakness and impulsiveness, I could not be awake while she was asleep, and I could not be asleep while she was gone. Waiting in bed, I listened for my mother's footsteps sauntering or scuffling up the street from the streetcar stop. There was her voice, singing too loud, trying desperately to proclaim and hold onto joy. Finally the key in the metal gate, the creak open and the pull close of metal against metal, now the key in the inner door, the swish and turn of the lock releasing, the door opening, the outside coming in. Now my worry could turn to anger, and the blessed arguing could begin.

CHAPTER 9
ESCAPE TO THE IVY LEAGUE

In high school, I continued the shame-by-day, anger-by-night pattern I had started in junior high school. I had been admitted to the gifted high school, what would technically be termed a "magnet school for academics," a public school that was as desirable as any of the city's private high schools. It was here that I began to mingle with the true upper classes, kids who'd gone to private elementary schools and lived in houses that appeared in magazines, whose mothers owned art galleries and whose fathers owned professional sports teams. For a while, I was able to channel my anger into ambition, into courteous but fierce competition for grades, awards, trophies, elected offices, test scores, and teacher recommendations. I entered speech tournaments and traveled up to one competition's statewide finals in a limousine, bringing along my best friend to accompany me rather than ask my parents, whose standard answer—"You don't really care if I go, do you?"—caused me to no longer ask. I went to school dances and after-school parties; snuck into clubs to hear rock and punk bands; tried out beer, Quaaludes, and mushrooms. And though I was friends with lots of boys, I had no boyfriends—my armor was too thick and my focus on achievement was too strong.

Success went to my head and I started to feel invincible. In a reverse kind of snobbism, I felt compelled to teach the Haves a lesson, to show them that I could outshine them at their own game. When it came time to apply to college, I snubbed my nose at the University of California, an excellent, well-respected system practically free to state residents and the destination for all the sensible middle-class kids. As a poor kid, I should have been elated to attend the UC. Instead, I applied to and was accepted into one of the most prestigious universities in the country—and certainly the trendiest, with John F. Kennedy, Jr. among the student body, as well as various DuPonts and Rockefellers and royalty of tiny, oil-rich countries in the Middle East. I had the audacity to buy a one-way ticket and fly east with a suitcase and a backpack. Then I took the train from New York to New England and caught a cab up College Hill to a campus I had never seen, a campus that looked like a park dotted with quaint brick buildings that were actually covered in ivy, a campus that looked nothing like the state college where I had spent part of my childhood. And I settled into a dormitory room as if I was going to glide through life from here on out.

Shortly after I arrived, I watched my roommate throw her typewriter into the trash can because the space bar was sticky, then call Daddy for money to replace it, and use the money instead for a half-gram of cocaine and a plane ticket for a weekend in St. Bart's, Tortola, or some other island I'd never heard of. I had arrived without a typewriter—I hadn't known one was necessary—and had no choice but to take hers out of the garbage, clean its keys with alcohol and Q-tips, and write my name in black magic marker over her monogram. That semester, my body walked across the pristine campus in crisp autumn temperatures to attend lectures followed by receptions with platters of spice cookies and glass pitchers filled with fresh apple cider. My mind produced papers and exams and pored over books till one in the morning when the library, named after John D. Rockefeller, finally closed. But some vital part of me—the part that houses my conviction—never made it across the Ivy line. Once again they had let me in, but I was getting tired of sucking in my stomach and holding my breath, trying to make myself fit.

And so the anger, for so long turned inward, toward myself and my family and the exasperating unfairness of my circumstances, began to turn outward. My pride swelled in an attempt to erase years of shame. It was these coddled rich kids who were from the wrong side of the line, I began to believe, and I who was from the right—indeed the *righteous*—side, for I had earned every single thing I had. But the pride that comes from anger is hardly better than anger itself. It's a tenacious little beast that swings you around by the tail until it burns itself out. Then it leaves you stranded, paralyzed, unable to think or speak or even see clearly. It breaks you down and drops you off at square one, except there is no more square one because you left it years ago, abandoned and destroyed your own home with your anger. You no longer have anywhere left to go.

In high school, I'd believed that if I could just get away from my mother, I could escape her way of seeing the world as if it were closed off to her, clamped down tight. But vision, of course, is hereditary. When I entered the foreign country of the Ivy League, even my vivid imagination was stretched to capacity with the extravagant norms suddenly surrounding me. Not everyone was fabulously wealthy, but even the middle-class kids had an understanding and an unshakeable faith in the rules of the game. They knew how the world worked and what to do to get ahead. An education was a commodity, a product that you (or rather, your parents) purchased, utilizing student loans if necessary, because after you graduated, you'd enter a profession and cash in that diploma for progressively higher-paying jobs, while also trading in your student loans for auto loans, mortgages, and home equity lines of credit. These people believed in progress the way my mother believed in luck. Success didn't come in windfalls for them; it came in steps, and they had either been born or bred with the confidence necessary to take those steps.

But I was my mother's daughter. I had been infected from an early age with a belief in the power of the one fell swoop, in the miraculous rescue by helicopter, in the quick and sudden flight from the street corner to the hot white circle of fame where everything would finally be perfect. Like my mother, I survived day-to-day on the fumes of that fantasy. I knew the motions and went through them, fooling everyone with my confident gestures. But deep down I understood that it was impossible, that my dreams were too dreamy to ever come true.

My freshman year, I would ride my bike, Lightning—she was white, English, with the sloping bar for wearing skirts—after midnight, when few cars were on the streets, curving back and forth as if I were skiing down the wide boulevard away from the school and into the part of the city untainted by the college. Also after midnight, and also often inspired by alcohol, drugs, or exasperation, I would pound with glee and fury on the sticky keys of the typewriter that my roommate—who was out partying—had tossed out and I had rescued from the trash.

One afternoon in late autumn, I returned to the dorm after my classes to find the dean—gray suit, oversized glasses, concerned flat smile—waiting for me outside my room. This man had been here once before, to mediate between myself and my roommate, a tall blonde who one night gave her key to a drunken frat boy and sent him over to our room so he could sit on my bed, wake me up, and try to get me to be less of a nerd. At that meeting, the dean had jovially suggested that my roommate and I probably "had a lot to learn from each other." I don't think he was aware of the list that my roommate kept of guys she had slept with that semester, or that she frequently overindulged in cocaine, vodka, and fraternity boys who ignored her in the cafeteria when she stumbled in for breakfast just a few minutes after leaving their beds.

This November afternoon, with the sun almost down, the dean was more serious. He was here, he explained with a steady gaze, because people were concerned about my behavior, worried that maybe I was not sleeping well or enough. He'd heard about some outbursts and altercations; perhaps I was having problems finding friends here, or making the adjustment from home to dorm. He wanted to take me to the infirmary so I could get a good night's sleep, and then see one of the doctors in the morning. He did not mention my roommate by name, but I imagine she must have read one of my late-night scrawls and misinterpreted my own energetic metaphors: *Lightning, here I come, to fly off the edge of the world*, typed one night in that uneven pica script before I went for a midnight ride down the hill. It was sweet, in a way, that my roommate called the dean, and sweet, too, that he came for me. But, except for sheer exhaustion and a general sense of being a stranger in a strange land, I didn't feel things were any more wrong than usual. The words "nervous" or "breakdown" did not come up, but they seemed suggested, and I began to wonder if they fit.

"I'm going to wait in the hall while you pack an overnight bag," said the dean, looking through his glasses and into my eyes. "But if you are not out in exactly five minutes, I will come in and get you."

He pulled something from his pocket and held it in front of my face. It was a key to my door, which he would use "if necessary." Apparently, he believed there was a possibility I would slit my wrists or jump out the one-story window rather than let him take me away. But the infirmary sounded lovely to me. I was happy to have the dean walk me over there and check me in. I couldn't wait to get into a clean white bed in a clean white room, with waxed Dixie cups of water and a nurse hovering somewhere nearby like an angel, protecting me while I slept.

And indeed I did sleep well in the white sheets and blankets, with the pewter-colored radiator hissing in the corner. But I had hardly begun to catch up on my rest when I was roused the next morning by a short, rounded, gray-haired woman hustling me out of bed for an appointment with the psychiatrist. The light was sharp, and my head was still cloudy from the sleeping pill the considerate night nurse had given me. The doctor was an important man, said the daytime nurse (or was she an aide? she certainly was no angel), and I was lucky to be seen by him, especially on such short notice. A few years later, when I worked for a caterer that served drinks and hors d'oeuvres to the local branches of the New England aristocracy, I would meet this aide's type again, working as housekeepers and maids, the behind-the-scenes servants not presented to the guests, whom one blue-blooded matron (and her face really was so thin and aquiline that you could see the blue of her veins) referred to as "the Irish," as if we were still living during the potato famines. This morning, however, her job, which she wanted to do well, was to deliver me to the doctor on time.

But I didn't give a crap about making the doctor wait, and I was sick of being told how lucky I was—to see this doctor, to be at this school, to possess anything that I had in fact earned, not won, as if from a lottery or a will. I had not asked for this appointment, after all—it was made for me, and I was personally escorted to the infirmary by the dean of the college. Now, this morning, I wanted the sleep I was promised. In lieu of that, I wanted to wash my face, brush my teeth, have a cup of tea and a bagel. How was talking to a shrink going to help me when I could barely think straight?

The aide may have been gray, but she had heft. She lugged me out of bed, down the stairs, and into the office of the doctor. The well-groomed, well-aged, well-dressed white man in a well-made neutral-colored suit (navy? taupe? gray?) sat at his desk with his back to me. He remained sitting, though he did turn to indicate the chair where I should sit and to smile the official knowing smile of psychiatrists, the one they teach them in graduate school, with just the right balance of condescension and compassion to blur the difference between the two.

He no doubt asked what the problem was, and I— groggy, grumpy, unwashed, unbreakfasted—probably replied that I didn't know. And then we would have bantered back and forth a bit, with him trying to charm me out of my defensive belligerence. At which point I would have thought, *Okay, Mister, you want to know what the problem is; well, I'm going to tell you*, and then I would have launched into a twisting and many-tangented explanation of the world according to me. The problem, I told him, is dishwashers: I did not know how to use one, but this boy I had a crush on in the dorm had told me in passing that he didn't consider a plate clean until it had gone through one. The problem, I said, is geography and equilibrium; it's the contrast between where I come from—and therefore who I am—and where I am now.

Where I come from, I explained, as simply as I could, we didn't have wide boulevards unfettered by traffic, even at midnight. We had three lanes of roaring cars on the crest of a hill and small children from the projects making a game of dodging cars against the red light, an urban version of bullfighting. Where I come from, the father did not wear a suit to work and come home to drink Manhattans; he carried a hammer, a drill, and a pipe full of grass. The family members did not gather around the dinner table every night to eat meat, rice, and a green vegetable while bickering amiably amongst themselves; we grabbed whatever we could find in the pantry and shoved it down our throats, alone. Where I come from, the mother had not been allowed to go to college, and so she left home at age sixteen to join a traveling crew selling magazine subscriptions, and a few years later she fell in love with a man who reminded her of Bob Dylan and she began having babies. Before she knew it, she was a mother to three kids and she could see no way to get her education except by moving the family to a tiny but affordable unit in the converted army barracks of the married-student housing projects. It was an apartment so small that the father had to build a loft in the closet for the daughter to sleep in, hanging a piece of canvas over the threshold to act as a door; a place where the cockroaches and the size of the house and the discrepancies between the parents, who were much too young when they first got pregnant and married, finally took their toll. And when the mother experienced a burst of confidence in herself and in the world surging from no explainable source, she decided that divorcing her husband was necessary in order to get her college degree, write her poetry, dance the can-can on foggy park stages, study with Allen Ginsberg at a Buddhist poetry school in Colorado, and in every other way step fully into her life. But all that energy and optimism soon sputtered out. Her anxiety and her poverty got the best of her, and work and school were all the mother could manage. And the children, who had been getting themselves to school on time—or a little late—for most of their lives, who had been fending for themselves and sometimes for each other, finally grew up and moved out, in an attempt to thrust themselves into the world despite everything they already knew about it.

This is where I come from and who I am, I explained to the psychiatrist, who nodded with an impeccable neutrality the same color as his suit. And this, I said, sweeping my arms around me to indicate the whole brick-and-ivy-covered campus in all its glory, is where I am now. And thus I answered, as best as I could, his question about what the problem was. But I had invested the psychiatrist with a sense of relativity that he did not possess. I was a seventeen-year-old kid—half-hippie, half-home girl—who had been acting like a mother to my own mother since I was twelve, and I could handle anything and anyone who came my way: winos, cops, welfare supervisors, even college entrance interviewers for uptight New England universities. But suddenly I found myself in a polite

funhouse fronted with marble columns and other façades
of decorum, where the very sidewalks, uneven with cob-
blestones, felt shaky, and I was confused by everything
including the weather, which, these wintry days, would
look bright and blue from my window, only to be freez-
ing—literally—when I stepped outside.

I had landed in an isolated cocoon of middle, upper,
and filthy rich kids placed high on a hill above the rest
of this small, depressed city, and the contrasts to what I
knew as the real world overwhelmed me. On Columbus
Day weekend, I'd joined twelve classmates, taking cars
and ferries and car ferries to an island called Chappa-
quidick, staying in a "cottage" that belonged to someone
connected to a name I knew from my high school history
class, a home that was used only on vacations but that
nonetheless had enough beds that not one of us had to
sleep on a floor or even a couch. My roommate was part
of a group of girls who tallied and compared lists of the
boys they'd slept with. By spring break, this big-boned
blonde, who often clomped into the room as I was rising,
had fourteen on her list, mostly fraternity boys, including several members of the elite frat that counted John
Kennedy, Jr. as a member, though she was unable to bag
the big catch himself. She filled our room with stacks
of clothes—including soft cashmere cardigans in every
color imaginable, as if she had simply checked "all" on the
catalog order form—and came back to the room three or
four times a day to change her outfit before making her
rounds. Meanwhile, I went to class, and three afternoons
a week I rode my bike down to the local branch of the

public library to my work-study job.

Surely the doctor could see that I was experiencing culture shock, the jolt of being who I was where I was and then—bam—like a quick cut on the editing machine, with no slow dissolve or fade-in, the same old me in a new country with a new language and new laws. I was not trying to indict anyone. I was just trying to answer—in the only twisted way I knew how—the question of why I was here in this office, of what seemed to be the problem.

"So your mother did not really do a very good job of taking care of you, did she?" the man in the suit said, a statement posing as a question. Decades of schooling, from dancing lessons and Sunday school through prep school, college, and med-school seminars, and this man never learned the cardinal rule that any kid on the street knows by the time he can tie his shoes: *Don't you talk about my mama like that.*

"So you don't really know what you're talking about, do you," I said, a statement, undisguised. "My mother did the best she could with what she had, and she never did anything mean, to me or anyone else." I walked out of his office, pushed open the heavy wooden doors of the infirmary, and went to get a bagel and tea. Then I headed to class to try and learn something I didn't already know.

My problem never got a name, but it did get a solution: I was paired with a surrogate family, who would invite me to dinner once a month to give me a break from the pressures of campus life. The host family program was offered to all incoming freshman who came from far away, but I had ignored the initial invitations, just as I had ignored so many school notices over the years, as part of the "exclusion principle" I'd invented for myself in junior high. One student I knew, a sophomore, got a host family who lived on a farm and invited us out to camp by the pond in the mild weather and cross-country ski around it in the winter. My host family was a childless couple: the wife worked at the university; the husband, much older, was retired. The wife tried valiantly to get me to open up with her, as she drove me out to her home forty-five minutes away, then brought me back to school with her the next morning. But our visits were stiff, especially once we got to her house. A few years later, I ran into her on a street near campus, and she told me she was doing fine, now that she had divorced her husband. Apparently that awkwardness hadn't all come from me.

My work-study job, running after-school activities at the public library for kids whose parents were at work rather than home, got me out of the cocoon of the ivy campus three afternoons a week. I also joined the outing club for hikes in the White Mountains (such restrained mountains compared to the Sierras I knew from summer camp) and went out for rock-climbing and sail boarding sessions with other groups. And I made friends with all kinds of people, going to frat parties on campus and hippie parties at the off-campus co-op houses, and sometimes venturing off college hill altogether to check out a couple gritty rock and roll clubs located under the freeway overpass. I slept with a few boys from my school, but I always insisted that we were just friends, an arrangement that allowed me to never actually risk getting known, loved, or hurt. It usually worked out pretty good for them, too: There's nothing more desirable, I came to find out, than a woman who is afraid of attachment.

But, of all the things that this college offered, it was the classes that saved me. Just as in my junior high school, the classes in this school were also divided into classes. Middle-class kids tended to take the practical courses (engineering, economics, political science), while the rich kids hung out in the more esoteric departments (comparative literature, anthropology, something called semiotics, which was where they made films, though I felt like an alien there). One friend, the daughter of two physics professors in a state university system, wanted desperately to major in art history, but her father refused to let her on the grounds that it wouldn't get her a good job. By all rights, I should have been studying math and science along with her, or at least pre-law classes, laying the foundation for a better future, taking advantage of this Ivy League opportunity to pave my way out of my circumstances. But the offerings were too tantalizing—Classics! Geology! Spanish literature!—and I selected my courses as if I had a trust fund awaiting. For once, I saw the benefits of my parents' hands-off approach to raising their children: they appreciated learning for learning's sake, and had passed that impractical but impassioned value on to me. My classmates' parents, understandably nervous about the expense of this college, wanted to make sure they got their money's worth. But I was paying my own way with loans, grants, scholarships, and work-study jobs, and was free to squander my money on whatever alluring course caught my eye. When you don't believe in the future, except in fantasy, it's easy to get caught up in the present.

My excitement was sometimes tempered with what Kierkegaard, as I learned in my philosophy class, called "too much possibility," which made it difficult to feel a meaningful pull to one thing over another, or find a reason to choose one course or course of action over another. In fact, I'd spend my college career vacillating between the humanities and the sciences. First I'd revel in all the open-ended questions posed in my history and literature classes, then I'd seek refuge in the facts of biology and geology, which I pursued not for their practical value but for their very firmness, the way they answered more questions than they asked, promising truth and explanations. The history of the world and the evolution of everything was what I wanted to study, though I ended up majoring in anthropology, which supported my curiosity about how humans came to be how we are, and which also allowed me to earn a degree by taking only eight courses in the department, so I was free to study elsewhere as well. But I stayed away from semiotics, which was even more conceptual, and thus more frightening, than literature. Or maybe I just didn't understand it—the joke was that even people who majored in it couldn't tell you what semiotics meant. In any case, I pushed aside my dreams of filmmaking as childish aspirations and tried to concentrate on more serious subjects.

Kierkegaard had a melancholia to suit every mood, and when I wasn't infected by his "despair of possibility,"

I could get overwhelmed by its opposite, the "despair of necessity," in which the possibilities seem to all close up and merge with my own exclusion principle. That first year, I'd call my father often, to tell him of these despairs, mine and Kierkegaard's, and also to tell him about Thucydides and Lope de Vega and Rousseau. Yes, he said, he knew these names and their ideas and he knew these despairs, too. When he'd first gone off to college, leaving Brooklyn for Ohio, he had once written down his own energetic plea: "Good God, give a man something to do." For my part, I just kept signing up for classes, and they gave me plenty to do.

Christmas, I went home, but spring break I stayed in the dorm, alone, while everyone else either went home or flew off to a warm-weather vacation in Florida or the Caribbean. The campus was eerily empty without students and faculty, reduced to the regular working staff going in and out of their offices. But I had a research paper to write for my urban American history class, and planned to spend my time at the library and on my bike, racing down the wide avenues in daylight and in dark, the chilly April wind pumping life into me. Since the cafeteria was closed, I spent the days leading up to the break hoarding food, storing it in my room and in the fridge in the dorm lounge at the end of the hallway. I snuck out apples, oranges, pears, cheese, pieces of bread, and, from the salad bar, filled plastic containers with garbanzo beans, hardboiled eggs, and slices of broccoli, cucumbers, ham and turkey.

Garbanzos have a distinctive way of going bad: They get slimier in increments, so you're not quite sure if something is wrong until the end of the week when you open up the container and the stench is so overwhelming that you realize you must have been eating spoiled beans for days and that's why you had to take all those trips to the bathroom. It's a smell and a realization that puts you off garbanzos for several years. Otherwise, I was able to make the food last the whole break.

Back in San Francisco, the summer after my freshman year, I got a call from one of my roommate's boyfriends, a guy from the Upper East Side who played on the college tennis team and who had some sort of job, through his father, at a Pebble Beach golf tournament. He had looked me up in the college directory as we classmates were encouraged to do while traveling. It was a cool, damp night, and my mother and I were in our ground-floor flat on 14th Street behind metal bars. We were in the front room, which was also her bedroom, sitting on her bed watching *Annie Hall* on the little black-and-white TV I had won in a public-speaking contest in high school.

"I know it's kind of last-minute," this boy said on the phone, "but I'm in San Francisco, and I'm wondering if I could stay at your house."

My first instinct was to stall him, to come up with some kind of excuse—the house is being remodeled, or a film crew is visiting from L.A. and all the bedrooms are full. I knew what kind of New York apartment he lived in, how a man in a cap and a uniform opened the thick glass door for him, and another uniformed man pressed the buttons in the elevator that landed him right in his living room. But then my mother, thin blonde hair, big, happy mouth, looked at me with excitement: *Were we going to have a visitor?* And I heard myself saying, "No problem. Stay as long as you like."

Feeling numb, I took the streetcar downtown to the big hotel where his airport shuttle would drop him off. We had ten dollar sandwiches in a deli in the theatre district, then put his luggage in a cab and headed toward my neighborhood. We stopped at my building, beige and brown stucco with black bars on the windows, and he paid the driver while I unlocked the gate and shoved his bags onto the steps. Inside, my mother would be sitting expectantly, her hair brushed, the red patchwork quilt smoothed over the bed in the living room. The bathroom door would be slightly ajar because it didn't shut all the way, and the two kitchen chairs would be pushed up against the table we used for cooking, eating, reading, and doing homework. I should have stopped at the grocery store, I realized; there would be nothing to offer him for breakfast except maybe a cup of tea with nonfat milk.

Then suddenly, standing there on the stoop surrounded by this boy's designer luggage, I felt the embarrassment evaporate and the wonderful joy of rage descend upon me. Years earlier, I had stepped off the perfect corner of 16th and Sanchez, leaving my brothers and our friends to shout "That's my car!" as toy-sized orange Porsches zipped out of reach. And in my pride and naiveté I had hoped, pretended, almost convinced myself that I could step into one of those fast, shiny cars and drive away. In high school, I'd sat in classrooms while they talked about Andrew Carnegie and Booker T. Washington, about the American Dream and lifting oneself up by the bootstraps. I'd quoted back what I'd learned, used the "chicken in every pot, two cars in every garage" line to win accolades and scholarships. When I was let into the Ivy League, everybody at my high school seemed to know about it before I did and told me how lucky I was. One girl presented me with a card and a check from her parents; they were so happy to hear the news. Then, once inside the college, which was more like a country club than a school, I'd met the rich: the flagrant rich, the stupid rich, the oblivious rich, and the radical rich, who shopped at the Salvation Army to irritate their parents and never had the cash to pay for our late-night meals at the snack bars, though they had their fathers' credit cards to buy whatever else they wanted. Shame and anger had been fermenting inside me ever since I'd first stepped into the gifted classes in junior high school. Now, as I stood on the grimy concrete of my front stoop, my shame and anger did an about-face, so that instead of pointing at myself and my family, they were aimed back at the people on the other side of the line.

This pleasant young man who played tennis and golf, who had very nice teeth and skin and hair, was one of the oblivious rich who had never met anyone who lived the way I did, didn't even know white people could live like this. He was about to have his mind blown, and I was suddenly happy to do this for him. I couldn't wait to see him stammer under the dim light of the hallway, wondering *Is this all there is?* I looked forward to watching him try to guess where the guest room was, to figure out to how speak in our language, to understand the way things were done in our country. The transformation of shame to anger was now complete—it had turned into a fierce, vengeful pride. I was furious for all those years of feeling ashamed of who I was. I couldn't wait to stuff all that shame into his winning and benevolent smile and cram it down his throat. *Welcome to my world*, I thought, as I opened the door and let him in.

Chapter 10
Stagnate

Over the next two months, more friends from college would make that pilgrimage to San Francisco, look me up, and ask me to take them around to all the places that had never held any cachet with me: the Haight Ashbury Victorian where the Grateful Dead had lived; the field in Golden Gate Park where the free concerts had taken place; the cafes in North Beach where the Beat poets had howled. My sparse flat and young mother—we were always accused of being sisters—must have seemed like one more stop on the tour. The visitors would gape and blink, then their eyes would settle back to normal size and they'd relax into my unsettling but intriguing life for a day or a week before slipping back into their own. By the time I returned to school in the fall, I had a bit of cachet myself.

Now that my older brother had enrolled in a rural college an hour from the city, my younger brother had finally moved into my father's one-room studio apartment. And with all of her children gone, my mother had to give up the Section 8-sanctioned flat on 14th Street, which was only permitted as long as two dependents lived there with her. She moved into successively smaller and more depressing places, and seemed to be shriveling herself, no matter how much I pleaded or berated. My father, meanwhile, had managed to buy a tiny piece of Land with a four-room cabin and room to expand. It was too late to rear his children in the country, but this mossy spot in the redwoods gave him a place to plant and build. He left his youngest son, still in high school, to fend for himself in the studio apartment, and spent most of his time in the cabin two hours north. I still called my father and my older brother frequently, especially when I was in a jam and needed to talk my way out of it. But there really was no home for me to come home to, and so I stayed east for most of my remaining college vacations.

New England, for me, was a foreign country, with its green summers and white winters, with its quaint restrictions on buying alcohol on Sundays and its harsh vowels, which forced me sometimes to just nod and pretend to understand what they were saying. I'd traveled abroad—to Baja on my own; to Spain with a university exchange program, then through Portugal, Morocco, Italy, Greece, and Yugslavia on a Eurail pass—so I knew the thrill of being in a place that held no personal history. Maine, Massachusetts, Rhode Island, Connecticut, New York: these places gave me that same thrill. Since I did not grow up with leaves or snow accumulating in a driveway, raking and shoveling were pleasures for me, not chores. And when I found an old wooden pair of cross-country skis in the attic of a dorm I lived in, I discovered just how much fun it was to go out into the cold.

—

My parents were not able to make it to the pomp and circumstance of my college graduation, and my explanation, to myself and to everyone who asked, was that the trip was too extravagant for them. Not just the expense, but every aspect of a trip like that—the arrangements, the planning, the purpose—must have struck them as outlandish, as something only other families did, families who were wealthy or foolish or sentimental. They were not selfish parents—they did not hold anything back from us in order to keep it for themselves—merely unimaginative; it was simply beyond their imagining to make such an excursion, or to see that it might be necessary or satisfying or even enjoyable. Though they had not seen nor spoken to each other in many years, my mother and father wore curiously similar blinders, and seemed to view their roles as parents as incidental. They had no malice, just an odd combination of high self-absorption and low self-esteem that made them grossly underestimate the influence that they had in shaping the lives of their children. They did not realize that by dousing their desires, they taught us to douse our own as well. It was the children in the family who tried at times to step in and rectify things. It was my younger brother who bragged about me getting into, and out of, this college; my older brother who had bought me a mail-order sweatshirt from the college's bookstore and given it to me for my high school graduation. And it was my older brother who had driven across the country with me at the start of my junior year, helping me to get my first car back east.

My college was located in a grungy New England city with a polluted river, Mafioso, and embarrassing politicians who put cigarettes out on their ex-wives' new boyfriends. Nonetheless I remained there after graduation, motivated mostly by inertia. My classmates were going on to the next step in fulfilling their great potential—graduate school or an internship at a Fortune 500 company, or at least a trekking adventure in Nepal. Back in San Francisco, my brothers had moved on to community and state colleges; my mother was living alone in a studio on a noisy Spanish-speaking street while continuing to work part-time in the city's schools and study part-time at the city's college; and my father had married a woman who'd lived with the Grateful Dead and Janis Joplin back in the day, and they'd moved permanently to the cabin in the redwoods. In other words, there was now even less of a home waiting for me at home. I had no place to go and no reason to go there.

So I accepted a job at the university's geology department, working as a lab assistant for a professor who studied 8,000-year-old pollen. My job was to collect, clean, and count the fossilized pollen grains, using a microscope to distinguish the balloon-like molecules of oak from those of spruce, fir, and juniper. Then the grad students— some of whom I'd just graduated with—would turn my counts into data on how cold and wet or hot and dry it was thousands of years ago. Though it intrigued me to be probing into the firmest of facts about the world and how it evolved, I really took the job because it had been offered to me, and because I did not have the wherewithal to ask myself what I'd rather do. One might think that after four years of immersion in an environment saturated with entitlement, some of that attitude would have rubbed off on me. But apparently nothing—not even the evidence of all my achievement—could alter my view of myself as a Have Not. The idea that I had the right, the privilege, the ability, and the option to choose my next step was still foreign to me, and instead, I took what came my way. My college had a history going back to the colonial era and had educated many of the people who had gone on to run our country and its corporations. But this illustrious tradition was no match for my family's own history, and for all I learned at this school, it could not teach me to ask myself what I wanted and then to go out and get it. Whatever gumption I had mustered up in order to get to the Ivy League was finally sputtering out now, a gas tank running on empty.

My job in the geology lab sometimes sent me into the field to dig into the earth with ten-foot sections of Plexiglas tubes and metal poles; there could be no experience more grounding than this, I hoped. Indeed, the immersion and exhaustion of those days filled me with a satisfying bliss. One summer morning, two grad students and I ventured into a swamp with our equipment to collect a core sample of mud. The swamp was not as moist as we'd have liked it to be, so it took a tremendous effort to get that Plexiglas tube to penetrate the hard-packed dirt. After attaching one of the extension poles, we clamped a wooden two-by-four across it to create a purchase, and then we gathered round the pole, found a place for all our hands, and pushed and pulled with all our might.

Around us, the swamp was crowded with spindly birch trees; it was still early in the day, but the air was thickening with a humidity that muffled any ambient noise. We barely talked, so our breath, synchronized and punctuated by grunts, was the only sound we heard. Progress was slow, and we went at it for hours, attaching another extension pole as we inched our collection tube deeper into the earth. We concentrated so hard on getting that tube into the ground that the swamp faded into the background and those thin trees seemed to disappear, as did my own body and my self and the bodies and selves of the two guys with me. For several quiet, ecstatic moments, all I could see or feel was our six arms on the pole, like the arms of one creature rather than three separate people. Unlike that frightening infinity I'd discovered as a child, this disappearance felt like a gain, not a loss, as if the three of us, by exerting effort together, had merged into one, and were, in turn, merging, quite literally, with the earth. Perhaps this is why humans dig holes into the ground; perhaps this is what my older brother and his friends were digging for when they stayed up all night making a hole in the Gatorville playground.

When it was over and we were hiking back out of the swamp with our sample of dirt, we remained unusually quiet, skipping the jokes and gossip and teasing that we usually had for each other. Something profound, perhaps even holy, had happened back there, but we didn't know how to talk about it, or maybe we didn't want to, for fear of ruining it.

That September after graduation, however, the dark side of infinity came back. As I walked to the geology lab from my shared apartment, I used to pass a patch of pink cosmos growing out of a little square of dirt cut out of the sidewalk. The flowers were tall and slender with lacy leaves and deep magenta petals, and for some reason they struck me as a radical act of beauty and resilience for the way they thrived in an island of concrete edging the asphalt street. But rather than inspire me, they brought me to tears. I didn't know what to do with these flowers, how to look squarely into their splendor, and then look away and go on with my meager life. I would sneak a peek and then, even before I blinked, a whiff of something— Cynicism? Hopelessness? Inadequacy?—would appear at the edges of my vision, dulling the colors of not just the magenta flowers, but of the cars and houses, the laundry hanging on the neighbor's line, my own skin and hair. It was the other side of infinity, the opposite of that bliss I'd felt while losing myself in the dry swamp.

Despair comes as a vapor, soundless, scentless. It has no heft. Like fire, its power is in its agility, curving in and around its target, finding the susceptible places, surrounding and then penetrating. But fire is proud, taking down its victim in loud bright flames, happily destroying everything in its way, and finally burning itself out. Despair, by contrast, is clever; it understands its symbiotic relationship with the host organism, and so never fully destroys, just seeps in and infiltrates until every nucleus of every cell is distorted with malaise.

My despair liked a sunny day, windless, a day warmer

than it should be, a day that would bring delight to most other people. It would hang in this air and then creep inside me so I felt a bit off, as if infected by a virus, but was not quite sure what was wrong until it had settled in for good and it was too late to fight it back. Soon, my vision would be warped, my head and thighs heavy, my gait lumbering. It kept both fatigue and rest at bay, so I'd wander through day and night as if sleepwalking through water. And I would wander. Around and around the house I'd go, trying to find something to hold my attention, something that felt important and necessary to do. I'd pick up the broom, the rake, the checkbook, the telephone, the pen, but the vapor had penetrated everything, rendering each object weightless and irrelevant. The lamp, the tea kettle, the books on the shelf, the notes I'd written to myself and stuck on the wall: all had been compressed from 3-D to 2-D, like flimsy cartoon versions of themselves.

Perhaps these balmy days were just conducive to such a vapor, which likes nothing more than to hang in the air, stagnant, waiting for an invitation to invade. Or perhaps something had happened to me on a stifling September day a long, long time before. Perhaps it was a day like this when my father left our house for good, or when a stranger invited me into his car and I accepted, only to have him take my head and try to push it into his lap. Most certainly there were Indian summer days in Clear Lake, when the rest of the world was back at school and at work and my family was still trying to find a place to call home. Those autumn days were still and dry, and though us kids tried to make games with acorns and apricot pits and clam shells, the tension between my parents hovered around us, and the pale brittle grass covering the hills seemed tinged with hopelessness, as if everything—the oaks, the blackberry bushes, the catfish scavenging on the bottom of the lake—had given up. Even our yelling sounded hollow as it echoed off the dusty hills. And then there was a day, and an awful night, at the end of August when I was seventeen, camping by a river with the man who was my first lover—a summer romance just before I headed off to college. He was twenty-five, with a motorcycle, a surfboard, and a guitar, but with no ability to reach out and comfort the girl lying next to him in a sleeping bag. When he rolled away from me, I pleaded, raising my voice above the water, which was splashing down granite boulders and upsetting pebbles and rocks. But the only response was from the river, the sound of water wearing down stone. And though we were lying at the bottom of the canyon, it was as if I had just been pushed off the top, and was tumbling, like an astronaut, slowly through space. Gasping for breath, I reached out for branches or footholds, even clouds, but there was nothing, not even gravity, to stop my fall.

In the year after my college graduation, I often felt like I was back in that canyon, a thick, hazy lassitude hovering above me like a hawk, threatening—and sometimes following through on its threats—to swoop down and bite. I did start seeing a therapist, a kind woman who offered her ear and her sympathy. But working was the thing that really kept that raptor at bay, and earning money was the only activity that fortified me. So I kept two jobs: weekdays at the pollen lab, nights and weekends serving food and drinks with the high-end catering company where I'd worked as a student. It was through this small company, run by a middle-aged couple who treated their employees as well and as poorly as they treated their children, that I became intimate with the kitchens and dining rooms of the larger homes in this small state. And it was in these homes that I came to understand that there were two kinds of wealthy people: those who worked for their money, and those whose money worked for them.

The differences between old money and new money, I soon learned, are both crucial and plentiful. For instance, tipping: new money does, old money doesn't—or if they do, it's a ten or twenty to split between the five-person crew who just fed them crab philo triangles, mini chicken sate with peanut dipping sauce, and pea pods that have been gutted of their real peas and filled with herbed cream cheese "peas" instead. New money remembers what it's like to work, sometimes offers to help you carry in the racks of dishes and the boxes full of food—though you must always say no—or carry out the empties at the end of the party, shoving a hundred bucks into your palm in the driveway, saying, "You did a great job, honey." Old money, meanwhile, won't know where her purse is, won't keep anything as gauche as cash in it, and will remain on the couch with the late-staying guests, jiggling the ice in that last glass, which you need to put in the rack and carry out to the van before you can go home.

As for drinking, new money uses mixers and garnishes;

old money takes it straight, or with a splash of water or plain soda, and, even more rarely, a twist of lemon rind— but never should any actual fruit or fruit juice enter the glass. New money likes the bar set up on a card table in the living room, where their guests can wander up and order their own seabreezes or rum-and-cokes. Old money likes you to set up the bar in the kitchen, out of sight, and wander around to ask people what they'll have, then deliver their glasses on a silver tray covered by a doily. Their guests drink scotch, bourbon, something called rye, and they order these by brand name ("Jameson and water, just a splash"), though the host rarely springs for brand-name liquor for his party. So you have to memorize the cheaper booze equivalents—Cutty is a scotch, Jim Beam is a bourbon—and make the appropriate substitution.

At mealtime, new money eats buffet style, while old money prefers a sit-down meal, which requires numerous black-and-white-clad servers carrying in successive courses on gold-rimmed dishes. Really old money wants what they call French service, with the plates set empty at the table—including a decorative charger whose only job is to hold the place for the actual dinner plate, and is removed immediately after everyone sits down. Then the waiters and waitresses carry in platters of slender green beans and creamed carrot puree, of tenderloin followed by the Sauce Béarnaise pitcher with a miniature silver ladle. The servers stop and bend down awkwardly at each guest; the guests twist awkwardly toward the platter and lift the serving fork and spoon, and attempt—with one hand, if they've actually been to France and know how this works—to pick up a slice of rare meat, a spindle of beans, a spoonful of puree.

Old money is also more apt to accuse you of stealing. The time I got accused, the client couldn't find some silverware the morning after the party. She called my boss, who had known me for five years and was pretty sure I wasn't going to stick a couple forks in my purse, but who nonetheless had to call me, a wisp of doubt in her voice. An hour later my boss called me back. The sterling had been found, no apology issued. Perhaps I had put the silverware in the wrong drawer after I washed it. Or perhaps this client, like the one I worked for once who had no idea where her kitchen sponges were stored, did not know where to look for her own stuff, regardless of how valuable it was.

The time I did take something, I never got accused. It was a tall blue-and-white pitcher, part of a tea set of perhaps thirty pieces, with cups, saucers, sugar bowls, and the rest. When we were setting up for the party, the client discovered a long, thin crack in the pitcher and tossed it in the trash. All night long, in between courses, I snuck glances at that lovely piece of porcelain in the garbage can, and tried to figure out how I could smuggle it out. I wanted to put it on my kitchen table, filled with flowers, a saucer under it to catch that slow leak of water from the crack. My purse was too small, but when I took the garbage out at the end of the dinner party, I wrapped up the pitcher, which I now thought of as a vase, in my coat, then got shivering into the van with the rest of the crew, hoping no one would notice.

But the main difference between old and new money has to do, once again, with vision. Old money literally did not see me when I was dressed in my black skirt and white blouse, even when they were looking right at me, telling me what drink they wanted me to bring them or how they took their coffee. I'd glide through the cocktail party with my tray, pausing to extend it into a clump of people without interrupting their conversation. A hand would reach out and take a shrimp on a toothpick, dip it in the cocktail sauce and I'd wait for the empty toothpick, then offer a small napkin—no eye contact necessary or warranted.

I happened to get introduced, one summer day on my off hours, to a middle-aged woman, blonde hair going on white, white skin going on red. We were at the beach club, which was named after the Indian tribe upon whose land it sat. I'd been invited there by a friend from college who grew up locally and whose family, like all the other good families in this area, was a member of this club. The woman looked me in the eye and smiled: I went to the right school, was a friend of the right kind of family, and, since she knew my first name only, she had no idea that I did not have the right kind of heritage. She also had no idea that I had spent the night before in her home, proffering trays of miniature food and large drinks to her and her guests. Apparently I did my job—and she did hers—so well that I became anonymous.

One Sunday afternoon I was napping in my stifling third-floor apartment when my mother called on the telephone.

"Hi, Frances?" came the thin questioning voice from three thousand miles away.

"Yes, it's me," I said, trying to keep my voice small as well, so as not to scare her off. My mother had not spoken to me for a year; she had not spoken to anyone in that time, not to my brothers, who lived a bus ride away from her, not to her professors at the university where she continued to take classes, not to her co-workers at the health-food co-op, not to the maintenance man at her new Section 8 apartment building. Instead she wrote notes on scraps of paper and did mime-like gestures to get her points across. The last time I'd seen her, I'd asked why she wasn't talking, my voice equal parts confusion, concern, and frustration. "My tongue hurts," she'd written, pushing the note into my palm. She had also given up on transportation, deciding that she would no longer take cars or buses but just rely on her own two feet to get her wherever she needed to go.

"Is it hot there?" my mother asked over the phone now.

"Extremely," I said. "Humid, too."

"It's hot in San Diego, too."

"San Diego?" I asked

"I'm flying there the day after tomorrow."

"You are?"

"Yes," she said. "My mother died, and I'm needed."

Her voice was no longer rickety; it resonated with purpose, and I kept her on the phone as long as I could, savoring every drop. Long after we hung up, I stayed on my foam mattress, which sat directly on the painted hardwood floor of my bedroom, looking out the window, watching the afternoon fade into evening and then into night. I wondered if this stagnant humidity would break overnight into a rainstorm, or if we'd have to wake up to it again one more day. I wondered also if that resonance in my mother's voice was the sound of malaise lifting, and if it would soon be lifting from me, too. Along with the awe and the relief, however, a beat of resentment was also pulsing through my organs and out to my limbs. I had needed my mother, too. But she had not been able to break her silence or get on an airplane for me. She had not been able to do so many things I'd needed her to do. And now, for the sake of a dead woman—a woman she had not seen or called or written for a decade—she had jolted herself back to the land of the living?

Soon, however, my anger gave way to sadness, for all the things my mother had not received from her mother and was therefore unable to give me. I imagined a chain of mothers and daughters, going back to tenements in Queens and towns in Poland, each demeaning the next generation and trying so hard to keep her in her place. Curled into myself on the mattress, I cried deep, doglike howls and whimpers late into the night. I cried until I was hoarse and dry and empty. And then I was done crying, and the relief came back and filled me up again. Against so many odds, my mother had saved herself. Not only that, but she had broken the chain. She had, in her quiet, determined way, put her hand up in the "stop" position, and treated herself and then her daughter as if we were worthy and capable, as if we had dreams and the right to pursue them. My grandmother had not allowed my mother to apply to college, and when my mother finally had enrolled, she was one of the first people in her family's history to do so. And then she raised a fierce girl like me, off to the university without a hesitation.

I would like to say that next the night rumbled; that lightning sliced through the sky, releasing the moisture that had been weighing us down for days. But I can't recall whether it rained that night or not. I can only remember the relief.

The next day I was back in the lab, where I was discovering that the firm facts of the world we were digging up were perhaps not so firm or intriguing after all. Actually, the facts still fascinated me, but the getting of them was proving to be most tedious. I had fantasized about excavating bones in Africa, dusting them off with a fine brush and discovering the clues to the evolution of our species. But science, like everything I encountered, was not living up to my fantasy version of it. Though I got to go out on fieldwork excursions occasionally, I spent most of my time in a windowless, airless room, looking down a microscope, with one hand on the focus knob and the other writing tick marks on a checklist: pine, oak, juniper. Meanwhile, outside, a world was turning round without me.

Chapter 11
Get Backstage

After two years in the lab, word came along that a local filmmaker was shooting a low-budget feature in our city, and a friend of mine was catering the movie—again, low budget: mostly lasagna and garlic bread, which she made in her apartment. The movie centered on the local music scene, and much of it was filmed at a notoriously filthy rock-and-roll club named after an Elvis Presley song. This, however, was all it took to wake up my old movie-making fantasies. Soon I was quitting my lab job, steady pay check, and health insurance for a part-time job with almost-volunteer wages helping my friend cook and serve the film crew for eight weeks of shooting. I wasn't sure if this was an empowering step toward realizing my dreams or a giant step backward into financial insecurity. All I knew was that I had to get out of the lab and I wanted to be near that camera and all the commotion that surrounded it.

An older woman who had spent much of her working life in labs had recently looked at me with astonishment when I told her that I worked in one, too. We were taking a fiction-writing class in night school, and had just finished reading our short stories aloud. "You don't belong in a lab," she told me. "You belong with artists."

The artists turned out to be buffoons, but it was still good to be among them. Watching from the sidelines of the movie set, I began to realize that, like me, most of these people—the director, the producer, the script girl—did not quite know what they were doing. The difference was that they did not let their ignorance hold them back. Much of the movie was filmed in the rock-and-roll club with local bands, bartenders, and drunks all playing themselves. It was like an eight-week party, though on the sidelines I could see the producer—the guy who owned the club and had borrowed against it to finance the movie—arguing with the writer/director, his soon-to-be ex-best friend. When filming ended, I cooked fulltime at the catering kitchen, making smoked bluefish pate and beef tenderloin with two hundred-year-old port sauce for the blue-blooded citizens of the state and chicken artichoke casserole for the not-so blue bloods.

I also volunteered in the editing room of the rock-and-roll movie, and soon started dating the director, an older man (almost 40) prone to depression and obsessive-compulsive behavior who had no idea how to end his movie. One night when I was out late catering a party, he left six messages on my phone machine wondering where I was and if I was all right. Prior to this I'd never had anyone worry about me or my whereabouts, and I guess I was finally ready to give attachment a try. He was large-framed, not heavy, and he dragged himself around as if his own weight was too much for him to bear. Yet he was sensitive and trustworthy, and he liked my words and my ideas, even the odd tidbits I'd share about my past. We would spend hours writing, rewriting, and sometimes even filming possible conclusions to his movie—all of which only further aggravated the producer, my new boyfriend's now ex-best friend.

Still, that producer and his booking agent hired me occasionally to cook meals for the bands that came to play the club. Once, for a Ziggy Marley concert, I got paired to cook with a white woman who dated a black dreadlocked man, and therefore was supposed to know what Rastafarians liked to eat. Just before dinner, I got word that Ziggy wanted to see the cook in his dressing room. Suddenly my partner was nowhere to be found, so I went in alone.

The room was crowded, and I wasn't sure which one was Ziggy until I heard a voice, cool, flat, but commanding.

"What you serving for dinner?" he asked. He was probably not much older than me, but he was the son of Bob Marley and carried himself accordingly.

"Baked cod, stir-fried vegetables, and rice," I said. "White *and* brown rice," I added, hoping the thoughtful array of choices might please him.

"Do the fish have scales?" he asked.

"What?"

"Scales," he said, exasperation creeping into the monotone. "Do the fish have scales?"

Suddenly I was brought back to those *afterschool* hours of junior high, when a couple black kids would try to corner the little white girl and toy with her just for fun.

The most important thing was to not show fear, because then they knew they had you, and the abuse could turn physical. So I kept my gaze steady as I tried to conjure up a picture of a cod into my mind, only to realize that I had never seen one that wasn't boned, filleted and sitting in the refrigerator case at the grocery store. Then I tried to discern, from Ziggy's face and voice, which answer he wanted, whether scales were a good thing or a bad thing. His whole crew—musicians, relatives, and roadies—was standing behind him now, waiting for my response, and I was ready to give the fish scales or take them off, just to end this conversation and get out of this room. Maybe this was a trick, I thought: don't *all* fish have scales? And then it came to me that those catfish we used to catch at night off the pier on Clear Lake had skin instead of scales, that we loved this fish for how easy it was to clean, but that my father had explained that in his youth, his kosher family would not have allowed him to eat it. *They're bottom-feeders*, he'd explained, *scavengers*, and Jews considered them not fit for consumption. I'm not sure if I knew at that moment in the dressing room that the Rastafarians considered themselves a lost tribe of Israel, and that they followed dietary laws that were close to kosher, but I thought I'd found the right answer to Ziggy's question.

"Yes," I said. "They've got scales.

"Okay," he said, his mouth widening into a grin. "Go on, now." And like that, I was dismissed.

Soon I stopped dating the filmmaker, a depressed older man, and starting going out with the club's booking agent, a happy older man, thirty-six years old to my twenty-five, quick witted and street smart, though not much for book-learning. The new boyfriend was a manager for a small but acclaimed roster of national music acts, and also booked shows for the rock-and-roll club featured in the movie that could not find a conclusion. When the movie's producer heard that I was ending my relationship with the plodding film director, he commiserated with me. "I understand, Frances. You need a guy who brings you flowers, not one who brings you books," he said. Still, he pleaded with me to postpone the break-up, fearing it might send the director into a depressive episode and render him even more unable to finish the film. But I was ready to move away from stagnation—my own and his—and to see what it was like to be with a man who was not just trustworthy but also exciting. A man who brought me disheveled magenta peonies from his father's garden and left bottles of expensive shampoo on my doorstep because he'd peeked in my shower and seen the cheap stuff I bought for myself. A man who adored my body and my mind and who could undo what all the nasty and leering men had done to me in my childhood.

Indeed, layer by layer, my new boyfriend helped me uncover the parts of my body that were made for pleasure. We could not keep our hands off each other; we made love in parking lots and golf courses, in the ocean waves and then, after discovering water bugs in our bathing suits, again in the showers we snuck into at the beach club. At the end of one particularly long, wet, sandy day, he drove me back to my apartment, an ugly first-floor

flat in a neighborhood of sour-colored double- and tri-
ple-decker homes divided into apartments for pale white
people who had no cars to bring them to the beach. A
yellowy panic began to take hold of me even before I got
out of the car. It was a hot moist night, windless, and I
couldn't let him go until he knew the other part of me, the
part that was not laughter and skin. So I sat him on my
living room floor and then sat beside him with one of my
journals, reading aloud a particularly graphic description
I'd once written while in full despondency. He did not
understand what I was talking about—the vapor, the canyon, the feeling of tumbling slowly through dark infinity—but unlike my first lover in the riverside canyon, he
sat there on my bare, painted floor without squirming as
I went over all the gory details. No man had ever been
willing to listen to me describe this shaky ground without
rolling away, sitting on the other end of the couch, opening a beer, or turning on the TV. But this man listened, if
not fully comprehending, and was not deterred.

I moved in with him soon afterwards, and it was a
sweet four or five years of playing and loving before the
differences between us (age, reading lists, ambitions)
became too large to overcome. But in the meantime he
introduced me to a whole host of decadent pleasures,
including *backstage*, a time and place as suspended as
afterschool, but not nearly as dangerous. My work was
temporary and intermittent—catering, making cable TV
commercials, driving around New England collecting tax
bills for a mortgage company, casting extras for a Japanese
car ad—so I could often find the time to get backstage.

The thing about meeting famous people is that there really is not much to say to each other. You're nervous, they're bored, and even if they're friendly, there's not a lot of common ground to feed a stimulating conversation. Through this boyfriend, I'd meet Elvis Costello, Natalie Merchant, Michael Stipe, Leonard Cohen, and a peppermint-Schnapped Gregg Allman. At a street-corner flea market in New York City once, he recognized Doc Pomus, who wrote a slew of early rock-and-roll classics, and was now in a wheelchair, gray-haired and alone except for an aide. "Go tell him you're a big fan," my boyfriend said, nudging me toward the wheelchair, knowing how much it would mean to the old man to have a young woman remember him. I'd eat dinner with Bonnie Raitt several times, before and after she hit the big time, and dance at Keith Richards' record release party for his solo album. I have a picture of myself with an old friend from San Francisco, both of us sweaty in jeans and T-shirts, with Richards between us, his arms over our shoulders. He'd approached us on the dance floor—everyone else at the underground club was too cool to dance—and shouted out with a grin, "You look like I did when I was cutting the album." But still there was nothing to say except "Thank you," and "It's great," and go back to dancing while he went back to the models and musicians dressed in black and standing on the sidelines smoking. I sat in a cold van outside a rented hall in upstate New York one winter night, passing around a joint with the jazz greats in Sun Ra's band who couldn't get high in front their band leader. And I answered the phone once in the middle of the night at my boyfriend's house, only to receive an earful of cussing from one of those same band members who was passing on complaints about the club or the meals or the motel from "Sunny" himself. Another time I tried to make conversation, in Spanish, with Los Lobos in their dressing room. "*Mucho gusto a conocerte,*" I said, extending my hand to the one gringo member of the band who spoke only English.

The best times were on the road with the great Zydeco accordionist Boozoo Chavis and his band, which was made up mostly of his sons and chaperoned by Miss Leona, his wife. The Chavis family spoke a French-English patois and had a ferocious affection for each other that could erupt at any moment into a fight or a laugh. They'd shout at each other in the van, at the dance halls, at the late-night diners after the shows, at their home in Lake Charles, where they invited us one sultry afternoon for spicy boiled crawfish and tall cans of Budweiser. In 1955, Boozoo had a big hit with "Paper in My Shoe," a song about having to stuff newspaper in his holey shoes because he couldn't afford socks, and he loved most of all to sing and talk about, as he put it in his tangy Louisi-ana drawl, "where I come from." The worst time was one night in Chicago, when I found myself backstage at Sol-dier's Field, seated at a round, white-tableclothed table next to Paul McCartney, who'd just played the last show of his worldwide tour. At our table, he shook hands all around and flashed that perky smile that was so much a part of his reputation, a smile that commiserated with the duress that anyone in my position must feel, a smile that seemed to say, "I know how hard it must be to meet me." But still, I had nothing to say to him. Perhaps I could have tried "*Mucho gusto a conocerte*" one more time.

If backstage was the hot, white circle of fame that I had conjured up as a child, then it was turning out to be quite the disappointment. How was this—overeager smiles, empty words of admiration, drunken stumblings and grumblings—going to save me? Like everything else I'd encountered in my life, including love, sex, pollen, and the Ivy League, the glow of fame was falling short of my deluded expectations. After a few years of hanging out backstage in boots and black miniskirts in my best impersonation of a groupie, I grew tired of listening and watching, of telling people how great their shows were. I was almost thirty, and I wanted to make something of my own.

Chapter 12
Kill Your Dreams

Working a 35mm flatbed film editor is like sitting at the wheel of a Mack truck. It's a grand machine, not in its elegance or intricacy, but in its sheer massiveness, its noisiness, and its bold, fist-sized knobs and cranks so opposite the polite little buttons and dials of the efficient but soulless digital equipment that has replaced it. When I was working on the low-budget rock-and-roll movie, I was like Alice in Wonderland, stretching onto tiptoes to reach the levers and thread the six reels: one for pix (picture) and two for sound, and three to take up the ends of each. But there I was, somehow, in the seat of power and magic. It didn't matter when the A.D. (Assistant Director) had yelled "action" or "cut;" I took the yellow grease pencil and decided—with a thick yellow slash—where to start or stop a scene. I rolled the film forward and backward, trolling for the crux of the action, the exact right moment to cut.

If I did not know where the oomph of the scene was, and whether I should cut away before or after the climax, I took a guess, marked it in yellow, then unrolled the film from the reel, slipped it under the knife of the splicer, then snipped the other end and pulled that strip of film out, taping it to the side of the flatbed with a piece of bright-orange masking tape so I didn't lose it or scratch it up too badly. Then I put the two loose ends together with a piece of editing tape, punched down to make the tape stick, rethreaded the reel, and finally cranked the levers to rewind the film a few feet before moving them to the forward position so I could see what I had just inadvertently created. Then, not quite satisfied, I added three frames back in at the end of the first scene so the cut came just as the guy is bringing his fist down onto the bar but before he starts to raise it again. Then—BAM—the next thing you see is a head-and-shoulders shot of a woman raising her arm to shove noodles into her mouth with chopsticks, and there is confusion for a moment in the mind of the viewer, which in this moment is me, even though I just made this cut. But it's a good kind of confusion—*When did that woman come into the bar? Wait, that's not the bar, where are we?*—that clears itself up in a second or two, when you switch to the long shot of her eating at the table in the loft—*oh, we're in the loft*—where we have seen the criminals already, plotting to blow up the bar.

I had been wanting to make movies ever since I'd made that first one in fifth grade. So after a bunch of jobs—lab tech, catering cook, archeology assistant—I'd quit them all to be a film freelancer. It was my boldest move toward my oldest dream. But working in the film production business, it turns out, has nothing to do with making movies.

The thrill of sitting behind the wheel and making the film morph this way and that way, then back again is not at all what happens when you work on a set in the art department or locations, or even the camera crew. You start out as a P.A. (production assistant) where your concern is making it through traffic to get the film roll to the lab before it closes for the day; or figuring out how to make an old broken radiator look like it is hissing steam; or talking the owner of a suburban home into letting a film crew ruin the hardwood floors, crack a few window panes, keep the neighborhood up all night with a generator, throw cigarette butts all over the lawn, blow a bunch of fuses, and tear off the branches of the beloved elm tree with a cube truck driven by an eighteen-year-old even lower on the production hierarchy than you are. But this, in fact, is what I do.

I sunbathe nude on a lighthouse in the middle of Narraganset Bay in Rhode Island on a blue-sky summer day so that if for some reason the foghorn decides to go off in all this sunshine, I can walkie-talkie the A.D. on shore to hold up the take for sound. I drive a renowned elder statesman of film around in a minivan looking for a run-down motel location with no highway noise and plenty of parking, while the director of the film bureau chatters away like a real estate agent trying to sell him on the virtues of the Ocean State. I ride in an elevator with Patrick Ewing, whose legs begin at the height of my head, in the Boston hotel favored by the NBA, then make phone calls in a suite I've rented for a commercial production crew from Japan, trying to locate the white baby grand piano that the art director has just decided he wants to appear on the waterfront for a 5:00 a.m. shoot the following morning. For that same crew shooting still photos of a young white couple in tux and prom gown on the Newbury Street balconies of Boston—this is America, they will tell Japan—I lie to half the city and even my mother back in California, telling them that this shoot is for "a calendar," as the Japanese liaison has instructed me, when in fact it is for a cigarette ad. I over-powder the nose of a sweating stewardess on an outdoor shoot during the dog days of August till the powder cakes up like batter on her forehead, nose, and upper lip. Fortunately for me, her voice, as she attempts to sing "This Land is Your Land," is worse than her face, and so the footage is unusable anyway.

I drive around New England with maps and a camera, looking for the real-life locations to be used for the "run-down apartment building," "greasy-spoon diner," and "stuffy golf course" mentioned in the script. Like a private eye, I go through the Yellow Pages and track down all my local contacts trying get a lead on sites that fit the description and are located not more than an hour's drive (time is money) from the hotel putting up the crew, and that also have a nearby parking lot (from a church, or supermarket, say) for crew cars and equipment trucks, and a nearby room (in a church basement, maybe, or the rec room of a senior center) where the caterer can set up lunch. Then I paste up my pictures into folders showing the interior, exterior, and reverse view and turn them in to the location manager, who gives them to the director, who picks one or asks for other options. She can't tell you what she wants more of, just that she wants "something more," and so now I am driving around looking but not knowing what I'm looking for.

Then I'm offering a thousand dollars to the absentee landlord of the "apartment in a ramshackle house" for a week of filming, assuring him that this is the top rate and the disturbance will be minimal, though he doesn't much care as it's his Spanish-speaking tenants—illegals, probably, who won't see any of the cash—who are going to have to live with a film crew for seven long days. And the next day my insides churn with hypocrisy as I offer the owners of the "large, suburban home with wide, wel-coming porch and long green lawn leading to the water's edge" four thousand dollars a week, plus hotel and dining expenses for his family while the filming takes place. My memories of lawns and the families that have them are taunting me now, as I've just ripped off the poor peo-ple and overpaid the rich. But I've only got a moment to feel ashamed, because the crew is moving on now, to the "crowded block in a working-class neighborhood," where I go around knocking on doors to offer the neigh-bors fifty bucks to turn off their noisy air conditioners for an hour or park their not-the-right-era cars on another street. As word spreads down the block that I'm tossing out fifty-dollar bills as if they were two-for-one coupons, neighbors start blasting their stereos in order to get me to pay them to turn them off. And by the time I get the ste-reos and several car alarms turned off, and a barking dog escorted to a park a few blocks away, the hour of silent

air-conditioners that I purchased forty-five minutes ago
is up and I am beginning to understand the beauty of the
old-fashioned sound stage.

It's taken me a while, but I'm finally ready to move
away from my second home and second boyfriend to New
York City to work on more low-budget feature films that
would never see the light of a projection screen but go
straight to video. Other jobs include television pilots for
promising young comedians who won't live up to their
promise, sleazy made-for-TV movies helmed by directors
and crews who are trying to make the jump from porn
to legit, and infomercials with aging wrestlers hawking
combination vacuum cleaner/hair trimmers with sketchy
thirty-day money-back guarantees. I also work on several
vanity films directed by people whose only qualification
for the job is that they could raise three hundred thousand dollars from trust funds, life insurance, and relatives,
and thus were able to hire desperate rising (and setting)
actors and technicians to work fourteen hours a day for a
couple months, feeding them coffee, pizza, peanut butter,
and the occasional case of beer on those days that go to
sixteen hours. I sit in with an actor at the audition, trying
to read lines while his crazed eyes look intently, emphatically, into mine. And though he doesn't get the part, those
eyes do get him other parts. For years now I have seen
them staring intently, emphatically, on reruns of *Law &
Order* and other TV dramas. As production manager, I
get called off the set of the "downtown apartment with
bathtub in the kitchen" to talk to the two Teamsters—big,
burly guys, just like in the movies—who want to discuss

our trucks, which are being driven by twenty-year-old production assistants rather than by Teamsters. They say they believe me when I mention that my father is a union brother back in California (which he is), and tell them about the meeting I had with their local rep (which I did), how I showed their rep our meager budget and got permission to rent our two small cube trucks—one for camera and sound, one for grip and electric—and drive them around the streets of New York without hiring union drivers. But, they say, walking away, they're just going to check out my story with him, and if he doesn't back me up, they'll return.

And so now I'm living the life of a low-budget film crew worker in NYC, a professional aspirer in a city seething with them. I'm renting a room south of SoHo in the understated coolness of TriBeCa, living with a Finnish woman, a camera operator, in a loft that was once a sewing machine factory, just down the street from the TriBeCa Film Center and the TriBeCa Grill, both owned by Robert DeNiro, who lives in the neighborhood, as do Harvey Keitel and Willem Dafoe. I'm learning the art of staying in touch, of going out for beers in funky bars in the East Village or Park Slope in Brooklyn, of keeping your name and your face and your good reputation circulating among all the other low-budget film crew workers, of light gossip that entertains but never actually slurs anyone, because you never know who is going to have a handle on the next feature film that comes to town and you want them to think of you and your pager number.

Locations and Production require too much office

work, and I want to be on the set with the camera—my
first love—so I switch to the art department, to props and
set dressing. And now I'm learning the skill of the chronic,
low-level flirtation that seems to work like carbohydrates
for the crew of a film. I'm playing the part of the cute
prop girl, finding the right jeans-and-tight-T-shirt outfit that allows me to get the brand-new baseball mitt to
appear old by beating it against the sidewalk and rubbing
it in engine grease, and to look good while doing it, too.
I'm nodding vacantly as the grips, the ones I eat lunch
with every day, discuss with anticipation the "three hot
blondes in short skirts" that are mentioned in the next
day's shooting script and sure enough are ordered up and
delivered onto the set as if they were pepperoni pizzas.
I'm pretending to be deaf when the key grip—the one I
caught and then held for a long, quiet moment after he
tripped but didn't quite fall on a sandbag during a crucial
bedroom scene—asks his buddies which one of the three
they'd most like to fuck. I'm providing a humble smile
when the First A.C. (Assistant Camera) calls me "the perfect woman" because I have just diagnosed a broken CV
joint in the axle of the camera truck, brought him coffee
extra light just like he likes it, and also made flowers spill
out of a vase like summer in a jar on the "breakfast the
morning after" set.

Best of all is watching the D.P. (Director of Photography) press his face into the eyepiece of the massive 35mm
camera and then step back and turn in that way he does
when he needs me to move a prop or fix a painting that's
hung crooked. In exchange, he answers all my questions

about the tripod-mounted camera, that monumental hinge from which all other pieces of the set—props, actors, lights, crew—must swing. The first thing a director decides when she or he starts a day of filming is where to place that instrument, and the way the crew recognizes an inexperienced director is by the length of time he or she wastes trying to figure out where to take the shot. The D.P. lets me peek into the rectangle—huge, clear, like a bay window—and tells me how, just before he is about to shoot, he sweeps the edges of the frame with his eyes, to make sure nothing is out of place. And for a moment, I'm back in the San Francisco schoolyard where I first discovered the little window on the world in the Super-8 camera that made everything seem possible.

But then it's back to the business of making movies. The urgency of the film set—often of the hurry-up-and-wait variety—over-inflates the value of every job, down to that of the lowliest craft services P.A. setting up coffee and bagels. Every minute costs so much money, even on a low-budget film where the crew works for cut rates and the equipment rental shop throws in the clamps for free, that there is the feeling of being in a race against time, as if you were cramming for finals for fourteen weeks. This creates a state of constant tension that encourages people to do anything it takes—lie, yell, or kick the person under them—to cover their asses so they don't get blamed for wasting time. Outside, in the drab real world of New York City, grown men are sleeping in doorways, their bare toes peeking out from moldy blankets. Children are stepping over crack vials trying to get to school on time. Fires are burning and planets are swirling and flowers are blooming and dying. Inside, on the set, forty people are convinced that the bead of sweat that has formed on the actress's upper lip—*Where's Make-up! Get Make-up over here!*—and stopped the cameras from rolling, the lights from shining, the action from proceeding, is the only thing in the world that matters. And nothing is as fulfilling as the feeling of knowing with certainty what matters, and to be among others who also know this, even if—especially if—it is only a bead of sweat.

And then the job is over and the crash hits and it is no longer clear what matters, except the next show, which I now need like a drug and not just to pay the enormous rent. So I make a friendly call to people I don't really like and who don't really like me in order to find out what work is on the horizon. And then I'm on a job on a new cable series billed as the first Latino variety show, shooting at one of the big television studios in Queens. In the elevators I stand next to blonde models whose legs seem even longer than Patrick Ewing's, and in the lobby I pass Dick Cavett, the talk-show host from my childhood television-watching days who has appeared in at least one version of my cloud-fame fantasy and who is not very leggy at all. In the halls of the production offices, the show's writers—young white guys who wish they were working on the Letterman show—play hackey-sack while tossing around skit ideas, just like they've seen young TV show writers do in the sit-coms. I read their script, highlight the props in pink marker, then head back into Manhattan either by van or by train—choose your poison—to shop for "macho key chains," "six plastic rats," the "blind girl's cane." I buy fake things—like cloth flowers with dew drops made of glue—and doctor them up with paint and markers and spray-on sheen to make them appear, on screen, a thousand times more perfect than real.

It wasn't until I sat in a bar in the Williamsburg section of Brooklyn on a spring afternoon, drinking beer with my friend, the brilliant starving artist, that I saw my oldest dream for what it really was. Chances are, the tab was on me. Like most brilliant young artists, my friend had no money and no qualms about borrowing from me, though I, too, had very little money and was also trying to be an artist of sorts. Apparently I knew how to manage low-budget, freelance-work living better than someone like him, who was reared in an upstanding, middle-class black family in L.A. and got sent to prep school, then art school. Bold and charismatic, he was the type of guy who always lived in a not-zoned-for-residence studio and so always had to have a girlfriend whose place he could shower at when necessary. I was never quite a girlfriend, but he did use my shower from time to time. He was a painter, playwright, and video and performance artist. For one of his art school plays, I'd appeared in roller skates and a skirt and helmet made of cardboard, speaking lines in a gibberish that sounded vaguely German. Now we were talking, at this hip, grimy bar with the doors open to let in the air, about "making it." I had been in the city for two years, he had been there for four or five. Softened up a bit by the beer, my mouth just fell into a description of the helicopter fame fantasy from my childhood. It sounded so absurd when put into words that I laughed as I heard it aloud.

My friend listened and laughed with me. He had a robust, pliant body and a sweet round face prone to exaggerated gestures. He playfully turned his hands into a megaphone and stood up to act out the whole rescue scene, ladder and all, that lifted me out of my life on the corner of 16th and Sanchez and dropped me, in one fell swoop, into sudden, cure-all success.

"Come on up, Frankie; everybody's waiting for you," he said in a booming voice, as if he were the helicopter pilot.

"Here I come," I said, playing my part. "Get me out of here."

Then he sat down and had another sip of beer.

"You want to hear mine?" he asked. "I travel by limo."

"Limo?" It sounded so tacky, I thought he was still teasing me.

"Black stretch," he said, nodding his head. He was still smiling, but his eyes, through his rectangular Malcolm X-style glasses, were serious.

In his dream, that limo picked him up and took him to a series of parties in Manhattan. He was the darling of the moment, and a certain female patron of the arts was introducing him around as if she had spawned him. As he described the details—the clothes, the music, the drinks, the patron—my beer tasted suddenly bitter. How could this old friend and once-in-a-while lover who I truly believed to be a brilliant artist—and still do, despite the fact that he owes me forty bucks—be under the glittering deceit of such a spell? He created enormous sculpture-like figures; the only word, and it is a paltry one, that we have to describe these constructions is "puppets," but they were much less cute and more complex than that word could ever imply. Then he put these puppets onto actors and put them into edgy downtown theaters and on Wall Street sidewalks, in surreal and provocative performances about race and sex and art and everything else of impor-tance. And here he was talking like a rap-star wannabe. His dream of success was not about reaching people through sound and images, or shocking audiences into questioning their most basic assumptions, or grabbing the world and heaving it across the room. Success for him was money, fame, tuxedos, parties, and limousine rides.

But in truth, I realized right then, his dream was no more shameful than my own, which currently starred Harvey Keitel as the helicopter pilot. I had seen Keitel at my neighborhood diner, and so the latest version of the fantasy involved slipping my screenplay—not that I'd written it yet—into a manila envelope along with a note and leaving it for him with the cashier. Harvey would pick it up the next time he came in for eggs-over-easy, then call me to say how much he liked it and to offer to act in the film, produce it, finance it, whatever I needed. Really, the only thing the brilliant starving artist's fantasy had over mine was the limos. But for some reason those limousines—clichéd, frivolous, wasteful things—pulled everything into focus.

What, I wondered, did fame or limos have to do with the intrinsic joy of articulating a thought or a feeling, and

the immense satisfaction of reaching inside and searching outside for the right shape to contain that thought?
In my case, what did the "six plastic rats," the crooked
paintings, the Teamsters, the celebrities in the elevator,
the noisy air conditioners, the "three hot blondes," have
to do with the magic of possibility I fell in love with as a
child, with the power of surprise that comes when a moving picture morphs from one thing into another thing,
somehow creating a third thing that is greater than the
sum of its parts? What did my fantasy of so-called success have to do with the genuine satisfaction of creating
something out of nothing, an act that my parents, either
accidentally or on purpose, had taught me to love and
need? My original impulse was to express my feelings and
ideas in words and pictures, and that, I realized, putting
my beer mug down, not a ride in a limo or helicopter,
was what really made me feel full, potent, and alive. It was
a realization as commonplace as my fantasy, but it was
enlightening nonetheless.

"You want another one?" my friend asked, getting up
from the table and heading toward the bar.

"No thanks," I said. I wanted no more beer. I wanted
to run out into the chilly sunshine of springtime in New
York while there was still some daylight left in the day.
And so I did, leaving my friend to finish drinking alone.

When you are born poor, your needs are fewer—you can
survive on so much less than those born into plenty—
but they are also deeper. People like me need more pro-
foundly, more desperately, more extravagantly. We dream

of an adoring public, throngs of fans. We imagine ourselves as Michael Jordan. We boast and shoot the moon.
We run up our credit lines, banking on future wealth. We
walk like alley cats with our fur pumped up to make us
seem bigger. "I am the greatest," we say, trying to emulate
Ali. "Frances The Great," I paint on the curb in red block
letters.

Then we sit around waiting to be transported by an
outside force when we should be putting one foot in front
of the other to get ourselves moving. And this is when the
dreaming gets in your way. One kid from the 16th and
Sanchez neighborhood dreamed of becoming a pro football player and never quite recovered from his fantasies.
This was the eldest, and not the most cherished, of the
family with the four children and the belt-wielding single
mother who had no tolerance for the messing up that
was endemic to her oldest son. Years after we'd grown
up, probably even still, when one of my brothers ran into
him at the bus stop, he'd be full of the words and images
of making it, describing the training camp, the uniforms,
the teammates, when we all knew he'd just lost a job, had
fathered another child, had hooked up with a white lady
who was paying the bills.

This is when dreaming becomes a disease: when the
years go by and you are still sitting on the stoop, waiting
for the limo or the 'copter to come by and pluck you out
of your mundane black-and-white life and place you, in
one fell swoop, into the hot, white circle of fame where
everything is finally perfect.

"Hold tight to your dreams," we are told. "If you can

dream it, you can do it." But I say douse your dreams in gasoline and set them on fire. Or take a hammer and a crowbar to them. Do like we did with the grocery carts back in Gatorville and push them off the top of a five-story parking garage. Or just take them out to the side-walk and stomp them to bits. Kill your dreams, I say; kill your dreams before they kill you.

The rescue came by telephone, not helicopter. A call, from a friend of a friend from college who lived in a little town in southern Maine where I had spent many Thanksgiv-ings and Easters and Fourths of July. A mother of two, she was divorcing and needed someone to take care of her girls when school let out for summer. It was April, a few weeks after drinking beer with my artist friend in Brooklyn, and the windows in my loft were open to the noise outside. How would I like to come to Maine and live in the studio apartment in her house in exchange for watching the kids? The phone against my ear, I leaned onto the sill of my huge bedroom window and stared out at the narrow southern tip of Manhattan, and into the rooms and rooftop gardens of my neighbors, who all had nicer furniture and dishes and apartments than I did. It was rush hour, when things moved at their slowest, and the cacophony of bridge-and-tunnel traffic along Canal Street three blocks away surged up like it did every day at this time. Horns honking, brakes screeching, people yelling, engines revving and humming and coughing: it sounded like modern jazz, with the deep-throated car stereos beating out the bass line.

On the phone the friend of the friend, her voice saturated with optimism, was saying "beach," "children," "garden." In the lot across the street, a big union film crew was turning an empty building into a diner. They had been waiting for a sunny day to film a rain scene—the prop rain spitting out of the machine appearing so much more rain-like than the real thing. Today they finally had one. "Action on rain," yelled the A.D., then, "action on extras," then just plain "action," and Brigit Fonda scurried through the fake rain toward the 1/2/3 subway entrance, again, again, again. Then the A.D. yelled, "All right, cut; we got it. Let's get out of here."

The plan was to spend the summer in Maine, then, in the fall, return to New York and the movies. What actually came to pass was that one thing (including a boy) led to another, and I only went back to the TriBeCa loft one more time, in September, to pile my belongings into the neighbor's loft, then into the service elevator only these neighbors could access, then into the little Ryder cube truck—the smallest truck they make—and to drive it, without a Teamster, back north, where I moved into the studio apartment adjacent to the two girls and their mother. In this small coastal town on the southern tip of Maine, I put the dream to sleep, to give my real life, ripe with potential and disappointment, a chance to stir itself awake. I had no idea what I would be like without my delusions, but I was ready to find out.

CHAPTER 13
WONDER IF A WHITE GIRL CAN GET THE BLUES

It turned out to be my first summer in Maine, and it was my mother's first summer in Maine as well. There is no sufficient way to explain why she finally said yes to my invitation to visit, just as there is no way to explain why she'd always said no. All my life I had watched her vacillate between holding herself back with a debilitating lack of confidence and leaping forward with an impulsive overconfidence. This time, I happened to catch her in an impulsive moment, and she agreed to come visit me for the first time in the fifteen years I'd lived in the east, to see the New England she had only read about. Before she could change her mind, I bought her a plane ticket and coached her on what to pack, telling her that she didn't need to bring a coat, as it was actually hot here in August. Then, a few weeks later, I picked her up at the Boston airport, where she stood waving to me from the sweltering sidewalk, a proud yet sheepish grin on her face and a heavy bomber jacket under her arm. It had been so long since she'd left San Francisco that she didn't believe in a summer that required no coat.

In Maine, my mother and I wore clothes we'd rarely seen on each other: wide-brimmed hats and loose sundresses that draped when the air was still and swooshed when the breeze came up. We took the two girls I was in charge of, ages seven and eleven, to quaint beaches with ankle-sized waves, and rubbed sunscreen on their skin and on our own. We went blueberry picking, ate lobster, viewed the paintings of the Wyeths and toured the home of Longfellow. We tried, in other words, to taste this thing called vacation that we'd heard so much about.

Then we headed on a road trip to southern New England, where I took her on a tour of the key sites of my second growing up. After I showed her the trim grassy quads and ivy-draped buildings where I had gone to college, we went to meet the kind therapist who had helped me get through my twenties. I was not cured of whatever it was I had—how can you cure a person of her history?—but after a decade I'd finally become exhausted by the round-and-roundness of our conversations, bored by our voices saying things they'd said before. For many crucial years this woman had made me feel welcome and wanted, granting me the attention and concern that my family had not known how to give. But now I'd had my fill of the past and didn't want to wallow there any longer. I wanted to live in the present and lug myself forward into life. But first, the three of us, mother, daughter, and mentor, had to meet.

Understandably, my mother was worried about this meeting. She feared it would turn into an open session on her, two against one. But the therapist, kind as always, was reassuring. She opened her door and invited us into the small, warm room, where we sat in a triangle of chairs, very democratic, staring at the fire-colored rug. "What I'd like to do, if it's okay with you," she said politely to my mother, "is to have you talk a bit about what Frances was like when she was a little girl." Up till now, of course, the only version of the story that had been discussed in this room was mine. I had rarely heard my mother talk about my young childhood at all. "I hate to think about those days," she once told me. She was remembering them, I assume, as the days of a stifling and sometimes scream-ing marriage getting ready to combust, and forgetting that they were also the days of her children's one and only childhoods—days we could not and did not want to erase.

"She was a curious baby, smiling, taking everything in," my mother said, grinning at whatever memory had brought forth this description. "And determined—some-times too determined. She'd go after something, and I'd have to jump up to catch her and pull her back."

And with these tender reminiscences, both the offense and the defense got called off the field, and we were talk-ing and listening, my mother and I, without injury or intent to injure. Children, regardless of their age, love to hear stories of themselves when they were littler, and I was no exception. After a while, it was my turn to sum myself up, and I admitted my lifelong disappointment in myself, lamented my stagnation and my frustration at how everyone else I knew seemed to move forward toward their dreams while I stayed pinned in the same

spot, unable to believe in my inalienable right to the pursuit of happiness. Whatever achievements I'd made had
come through a slow sideways crab-walk, almost by hap-
penstance. I still had not learned how to state a goal and
then march straight toward it.

"I just wish I'd had a mother who showed me by
example that I could participate in the regular things of
the world, that I could have a good job, a decent house,
a family that ate dinner together," I explained, staring at
the therapist's curved leather chair. "I wish I had been
brought up by a mother who showed me that I could
work toward things and accomplish them, rather than
spending my life in perpetual yearning."

It was quiet for a moment as we all looked down at
the red and orange stripes on the rug. Then came the soft,
weary voice of my mother.

"Me, too," she said. I had not been implicating her,
and she knew this, just as she understood exactly what I
was wishing for. "Me, too," she said again. "I also wish I'd
had a mother who taught me those things, who showed
me they were possible."

We looked at each other then, our faces open with
recognition, empty of blame or guilt. For so many years,
we each, alone, though often at the same time and in the
same small apartments, had been trying to make our way,
to invent optimism and faith, to convince ourselves that
we were entitled—in the best, most literal sense of that
word—to dwell in the land of possibility. And so often
those parallel desires had erupted into yelling and silence
and desolation. What you don't get from your mother

you will crave for the rest of your life, and she and I were partners in this particular craving.

The room got quiet again, as the three of us basked in the glow of empathy. For a long, long time we just sat there under a halo of glee, cocky with epiphany, satisfaction oozing out of the upturned corners of our mouths. Then it was time to hug and say goodbye.

My mother used to tell me that love—the marrying kind—was her missing piece, and with it she would be righted, everything else in her life falling into place. If only she were loved by a man, she used to say after the divorce, then she would be able, in turn, to better love us, her children. And who is to say that she was wrong? Who is to say, as the old songs do, that the blues ain't nothing but a woman looking for a man, that love is not the cure for despair?

In the grungy New England city, before I had love, I'd turned to the next-best thing: psychology. The kind therapist I started seeing just after graduation listened to me for years. On one of these visits—I'd driven four hours from my apartment in New York, crying for no reason I could name—she asked me to consider trying a new medicine that had recently come on the market, one that seemed to work well on people with my diagnosis.

"I have a diagnosis?" I asked. Sure, "depression" had been tossed around in our discussions for years, but so had "fear," "resentment," "disappointment," and other feral nouns. But she assured me now that I had something called dysthymia, a mild, low-level depression

whose official definition was filled with slippery descrip-
tors like "occasionally" and "in some cases." Dysthymia
sounded like the irritable bowel syndrome of mental illness, a condition that hovered like a yellow jacket and,
every once in a while, produced a sting. But I could not
deny that the past winter in New York was the first time in
my hungry life that I had lost my appetite and that I was
also finding it harder and harder to make the calls necessary to get freelance film, or even, some days, to get out
of bed. And so I began to wonder if my problem all these
years, the thing that kept me feeling like I could never
fully participate in the abundance of the universe, had
been not poverty or solitude, not economics or geography, but biochemistry.

Certainly I did not have real depression, the kind
I'd seen in my first real boyfriend, the filmmaker who'd
had such trouble finishing his film. This man had all
kinds of diagnoses, and also had either the bad luck or
the masochism to rent mostly attic apartments in older
houses so that on two occasions, in two different apartments, he encountered a live bat flying around inside his
rooms, something that most of us do not encounter even
once in a lifetime—and if it does happen we do not drive
ourselves on both occasions to the emergency room and
undergo the painful, six-week series of stomach-injected
rabies shots because we can't remember if the bat bit us
or not, if in fact we even touched the bat as we shooed
it, with a broom and a baseball mitt, out the window.
No, whatever this man had, it was a distant cousin to the
thing I had.

But now, it seemed, there was a new disease, a milder, vaguer, more accessible form of depression available even to a Have Not like me. It puzzled me that this new disease—at least my diagnosis with it—seemed to come about only with the invention of a drug that could treat it. But rather than get all caught up in the wag-the-dog question of whether a cure had created an illness, I marveled at the possibility that all my problems—my anger at the rich, my fantasy of fame and escape, my trouble combining sex and love in intimate relationships, my sense that nothing in the world was actually possible for me—could be traced to the shapes and quantities of the molecules inside my head, molecules not much smaller than the pollen grains I'd counted in the geology lab. What a magnificent idea: the problem and its solution were scientific—concrete, knowable, describable, and not at all negligible. It was a chemical—or the lack of one—that made me think and live and talk in spirals, not the fact that I was lonely, had a broken family, and came from a poverty which started with a lack of money and then spread both outward and inward until every cell was saturated with a paralyzing combination of desire and cynicism.

Though I had an aversion to drugs—I might take them for recreation but drew the line at medication—I was tempted by the idea that they might give me my first taste of what it was like to be a Have. Around and around I went with questions about genetics and environment, and wasn't sorrow a part of being human and anguish the necessary burden of the artist, and whether I would still be stunted by malaise and anger if I had been born into a comfortable suburban home with a lawn and a fridge full of food. I tried to poke holes in my own theories, asking myself, as much as the therapist, how come some poor people managed to cultivate the open mind of the Haves while certain rich people with all the possibilities in the world moped around like Have Nots? Perhaps, I wondered, there were sub-classifications which I hadn't yet properly accounted for: the *Have-Not* Haves, those people gifted with money but none of the other things— trust, admiration, pride, responsibility—necessary for blossoming; and the *Have* Have-Nots, the rags-to-riches types who brushed off adversity as if it were a mosquito. Clearly, you didn't have to be poor to live in poverty, but it sure helped.

Finally, I gave in to my curiosity and set out to find a doctor who would give me a prescription. With no health insurance and relatively good health, I had no doctor I visited regularly for check-ups. Prozac was an expensive drug—perhaps this is why the kind therapist had hardly mentioned it to me before—but the doctor who agreed to see me for a reduced rate was able to give me a large cache of samples to get me started. The pill did not erase my despair, but over the next year or so it provided me with a layer of protection from the despair's intense and debilitating power.

Soon I began to wonder if my mother might have a diagnosis as well. During that worrisome year, when she stopped talking and taking transportation, her eyes had drooped with a sadness that clearly hurt, and which she tried to cover up with mirrored sunglasses, rain or shine, indoors or out. Then, just as suddenly and inexplicably as she'd stopped, she'd begun speaking again, started boarding buses and streetcars. People, such as my dance teacher on the streetcar, would sometimes ask, "How is your mother doing?" in a tone that conveyed more than casual concern. But no one, not my father, not my brothers and I amongst ourselves, had ever wondered aloud what was happening to her and if she, and we, would be all right.

Eventually I came up with a diagnosis of my own: My mother was not just a poet, but a poem, I decided—one by Emily Dickinson, who she'd studied in grad school. Cryptic and enchanting, she had a definite and intricate rhythm and something urgent to say about the world. But if you got too close, tried too hard to figure her out, she would fly off like a pigeon from the sidewalk, leaving you frustrated, with breadcrumbs in your hands.

"What is wrong with Mom?" I used to wonder, at fourteen, seventeen, twenty-five, thirty years of age. "Why doesn't she finish college, and get a career and a house and a husband, like she says she wants? Why does she seem most comfortable in the yearning position?" And then I'd stop with a sudden panic, and wonder who was I talking about here, my mother or myself. Though I never admitted it to her or anyone else, everything she did I could understand, in the same way that I understood poetry: fully but not thoroughly, in the body if not the mind. I could empathize with her every action but stopped short of carrying them out myself, and I didn't know whether to be frightened or comforted by this compatibility, by how easy it was for me to see why someone who had felt the pain of the spoken word, who had been criticized as a little girl and a young woman, who had shouted back and forth with her husband in front of and away from the children, who heard insults in many different languages hurled about each day on the sidewalk and in the class-room, would feel an ache in her tongue and stop partici-pating in speech altogether. Or why a woman who rode the bus for years at all hours of the day and night would finally get tired of waiting on windy street corners, fed up with people refusing to scoot their legs to the side so she could get out of the seat in time for her stop, or men rub-bing themselves against her backside, and decide to take her transportation into her own hands, or feet.

What was wrong with my mother was also what was wrong with me, only more so. I understood how she viewed the world as tantalizing yet impossible, how she exempted herself from the very physics of human behavior, how she waited for the lucky break while knowing in her bones that nothing truly good would ever happen to her; I knew these things about her because I felt them myself.

Years later, I would hear about a man who stopped talking and started walking as a form of protest against the destruction of the environment. He had a Ph.D and wrote a book about his silent journey, and was celebrated as an innovative, wise, and dedicated man willing to cross into new territories at great personal sacrifice. Perhaps, I wondered when I heard about him, my mother had been more ingenious than any of us had imagined.

Not all blues songs are about a woman looking for a man, or wronged by a man, or fooling hopelessly with a

married man. Some of those records wail in the deep, gut-
tural ache of a lone guitar and a lone voice, with a sadness
that sounds primordial, as if it started with the very first
algae and protozoa, then dragged itself out of the swamp
with the amphibians that were beginning to lay eggs on
land and eventually would become human. Perhaps at
the center of our universe and the core of our earth lies a
small but powerful gloom, which can be felt like a sound
wave only by those people gifted with chemicals or circumstances—or the lack of them—or those born with
empathic hearts or particularly thin skins. So where are
the blues, then? Are they inside or outside of a person?
And can a white girl get them, or does she get dysthymia, cognitive therapy, and Prozac instead? Is it only a few
degrees that separate depression from despair, or from
loneliness, bad attitudes, and plain-old wallowing in self-
pity? And what is despair but a kind of poverty of the
spirit, a scarcity of faith? Is it the difference between being
poor in spirit, as opposed to poor in money, a distinction
my mother, in all her brilliance, pointed out to me in our
iron-barred flat when I was a teenager?

I don't know if my mother ever got a diagnosis, or
how close it came to the one given to me. I was told I
had a mild form of depression, but I always wondered if I
could have received a diagnosis of poverty instead. It was
not just a lack of money that I suffered from, but also a
lack of love and attention, of safety and faith and confidence in myself and in the world around me. Perhaps my
brain was deficient, too, in serotonin, but it felt like what
was really missing was a sense of the possible.

After the session with the kind therapist, my mother
and I spent the night at the home of some old friends
of mine from college, then started off on a driving tour
of literary New England, visiting the sites of the legend-
ary authors we had both read, studied, and admired. It
was my mother, of course, who had first introduced me
to the pleasure and the necessity of reading and writing,
and our mutual veneration for the written word and the
writers who produced them was one of the sweet spots
in our relationship. On our tour we saw Thoreau's cabin,
the remnant and the replica; swam together in Walden
Pond; walked through Hawthorne's Colonial home. In
one of her self-confident periods, my mother had studied with Allen Ginsberg in the early days of the Naropa
Institute's Jack Kerouac School of Disembodied Poetics,
though I'm not sure we made it to Lowell, Massachusetts, home to Kerouac, whose working-class Catholic
upbringing reminded my mother of her own. But the
highlight of the trip was the Emily Dickinson Homestead
in Amherst. Timid in life and bold with her words, Dickinson had removed herself from the world, and I imagine
my mother felt a sisterhood with this withdrawn poet.

Waiting for the house tour to begin, we inspected
the rather bland brick home from the outside, looking
for clues to the life it had contained. Then wandered in
the gardens, which were lush but prim, English-style.
The afternoon was muggy, and the humidity was still
building, headed toward a thunderstorm later in the day.
My mother, in a long black-and-white gingham dress,

strolled past the rosebushes, the pink flowering dog-
wood, the blue spikes of delphinium, with a serene smile
on her face. When the guide let us and the two other parties into the house, we hung back, inspecting the table
where Emily Dickinson ate, the sink where she washed,
the balustrade she held onto when descending the staircase. Upstairs, in the bedroom, we saw the desk—surpris-
ingly small—where she wrote, and the narrow sleigh bed,
covered in stern white lace, where she slept.

"Look," my mother whispered, pointing to a window
facing the front of the house. "That must be where she
let the basket down." Dickinson, my mother explained,
liked to fill a basket with cookies, tie a rope to it, and
lower it down to neighborhood children playing outside
the house. It was, apart from her poems and letters, one
of the few ways she consented to communicate with the
world.

In front of the house—we'd lingered in the bedroom
till the tour guide kicked us out—I took photos of my
mother reenacting the role of the children who might
have gathered down below, hoping for cookies. She
looked up to the bedroom window and smiled at where
Emily must have stood, then reached up to take hold of
the imaginary basket and guide it to safety. Finally, we left
to visit the cemetery. Dickinson's headstone was humble,
of course, but adorned with offerings—candles, flowers,
poems. We had brought nothing, but my mother, whose
quirky brilliance was in full form that day, extracted a pen
from her daypack and left it on the worn granite so the
poet would have something to write with.

A few hours later, the thunderstorm struck hard with loud electric cracks and heavy rain. We had lingered so long with Dickinson that the day had become dark and late, as well as wet, by the time we got on the highway. The plan was to spend the night back at the home of my college friends again, but at this rate we wouldn't arrive until after midnight. We were exhausted and the driving was miserable; though my mother technically had a license, she rarely drove, so I was doing it all, and it was making me cranky.

"If only we could stay someplace near here," I whined like a little girl.

"I think we passed a billboard a few miles back that advertised rooms for forty-five dollars," my mother replied in a hesitant, almost questioning, voice. I glanced over at her—briefly, as I had to keep my eyes on the road—and we both saw something new in the face staring back. Staying in a hotel was something we had never done together, something I had done only with the rock-and-roll boyfriend who always expensed it, something I don't know that my mother had ever done in my lifetime except maybe once on a protest march in Sacramento where twenty people slept on the floor in sleeping bags. As a family we'd always camped, though when I drove across the country with my older brother, we did stay in a few youth hostels.

"Forty-five dollars. For two people. That's really not that much," I said.

"It's not." Her voice, though low in volume, had a squeal to it.

"Of course there's tax on top of that," I said, remembering my role as the sound one, and trying not to get too swept up in the excitement. I would be the one paying for it, after all.

"But still," she said.

"Yeah, still," I said. "And maybe there's a Triple A discount, too."

We drove on a few more miles, adjusting to the idea that we could be like other people, people who take summer vacations and spend their nights in hotels. It was as if a window had opened and sent in a breeze, and we didn't know if we should luxuriate in this fresh air or slam the window shut against it. But somehow we managed to convince ourselves and each other, because soon we were pulling off at a gas station, finding a pay phone, calling information with only the vaguest idea of the name of the motel my mother had seen on the billboard, and getting a number that got us a room with access to a pool and, yes, a discount, too. We giggled at our newfound audacity all the way there, and then continued giggling at the front desk, down the hall, and into our room, where we changed into our swimsuits and then went diving and splashing and floating in the indoor pool.

Two weeks later my mother was back in her government-subsidized, hot-plate-in-the-living room flat, racing to get to her two hourly-paid jobs on time, and I was back in Maine, trying to hold onto the summer's glee and conjure up my next move. I was waitressing and writing articles for local newspapers and regional tourist magazines, covering the kinds of things that beginning writers in semi-rural vacation areas must cover: art openings with paintings of flowers and sailboats, and flattering profiles of local chefs and innkeepers, as well as practical guides for do-it-yourselfers trying to choose a material (gravel, crushed stone, or asphalt) with which to pave their driveways. Part of me still hoped for the one-fell-swoop version of success to come down and rescue me from the stones and gravel and wispy floral watercolors, but I was trying to teach myself to start at square one. Like recovering addicts who describe themselves as "egomaniacs with an inferiority complex," I had to swallow my pride in order to move forward, step by step.

In many ways, I was now living the life that my father had always wanted to give me. I moved onto a family farm, into a room heated by a wood stove, and learned how to make fires, grow food, milk cows, and make cheese, honey, and maple syrup. And though my father still did not venture out to visit this country version of his daughter, he loved to listen to me describe it on the phone or when I came home for a visit. He was busy making his own country life with a cabin in the redwoods, bolstering it up with an addition, and rolling and wedging stones into walls and steps. In Maine, his California daughter learned to surf and row and sail, and then, when the ponds froze over, to skate on them, sometimes gliding alone, sometimes fighting with a battered stick over a battered puck using the flailing arms of the waterbug defense I'd learned in the schoolyard basketball court back on 16th and Sanchez.

And my father seemed satisfied to hear about, but not participate in, all the ways I was taking advantage of the world.

Chapter 14
Age Before You Ripen

Riding waves is one of the few ways I know ecstasy. My body tucks itself into the beginning of the curl—timing is everything—and gets hurled toward shore, sometimes thrown onto the sand and beached, the white water pulling back into the ocean without me. The saltwater seeps through my pores, forms my mouth into an incessant grin, and washes out all the nagging stuff inside my head. Today is a good day for body surfing: the waves are small but sharp, the water is not quite as cold as it usually is in Maine, and the nasty red seaweed is nowhere to be seen. But my little buddy—the youngest daughter of the divorced friend of the friend—has got no fat on her, and soon the water chills her to the bone. Her lips turn blue, and finally she runs up to our spot on the beach to wrap herself in a towel, while I stay in for a few more free rides.

We are celebrating her birthday and have the whole day to do whatever she wants in this genteel town in Southern Maine, a town where we leave the car keys in the ignition when we park and lift our hands off the steering wheel to wave as we pass one another on the road. After taking care of the two girls, I've remained best friends with the younger one—let's call her Angel—even after I moved out of her house. It's summer, she's eight or nine, and so far we have picked raspberries, eaten them in pancakes with whipped cream, and canoed on the pond at the farm where I've recently moved. After the beach, we're going to get ice cream cones and visit the stuffed animals at the toy store.

After a few more rides, I remember to look up and see how she's doing—even though I'm the one in the water and she's the one on shore. Funny that she's moved away from our stuff and is standing, rather than sitting, her towel draped around her like a cape. But my wave comes and I give myself up to it. A few more rides, another look up. There's Angel, walking back and forth at the water's edge, looking for shells and singing to herself. And there's a man. He's sitting too close to our stuff for how much space there is on this beach. I get out of the water.

We're drying off, putting on our sundresses over our swimsuits, when Angel whispers, "Frankie, that man is looking at us."

"Oh, it's okay," I whisper back, pretending like nothing's wrong. We're not in physical danger—this man is not going to hurt us—but his placement and his look are so intrusive that Angel's ears are up and back like a cat's, alert and on guard. I keep talking, about whatever, to distract her while we slip off our wet suits from under our dresses and pack our towels into our bags.

"That man is still looking," Angel whispers again. This time I agree, say that he's weird, but not to pay him any mind. But I quickly get us on our way, walking on the firm sand by the water, and talking about the waves and the rides we took, about the stuffed animals we're going to see at the toy store, about how much fun we're having on this blue and yellow summer day.

"That man," Angel says, trying to figure out what's happened—what he was doing, and why it felt so wrong, how come it seems like he's taken something from us without touching or even talking to us—"why was he looking at us like that?"

It's been years, lifetimes, since I got into the car with the man on the corner of 16th and Sanchez in San Francisco, but here on the beach in Maine he has returned to steal something from me once again. And I am as helpless to save Angel as I'd been to save myself in the schoolyard or the playground or the comic book store. Angel is thrown off. She doesn't understand that look he's giving us, though she knows it's wrong, and she can't let it go no matter how I try to brush it off. So now I am pissed off at this man, who is every man who ever looked at me wrong, every man who ever looked at any girl wrong.

I want to show Angel that you don't have to let them walk up and steal you from yourself. I don't want her to put on the armor, like I did at her age, and to grow up fearful and queasy about sex and her body, suspicious of men and love and pleasure. My parents had made a mistake with me—tried to pretend it didn't happen—and I don't want to make the same mistake with Angel. If she can't ignore it, then neither can I. So I walk back a few paces to where the man is sitting, and I tell him that he made us feel very uncomfortable. In my experience, simply confronting the man in a polite but firm voice and with unwavering eye contact often shames him into leaving, sometimes even apologizing.

But this man on the beach gets angry rather than ashamed or apologetic. He denies any wrongdoing. He yells. I yell back, repeating myself: We didn't like the way he was looking at us. Then I join up with Angel, who has witnessed the whole outburst and is now shivering with nausea and worry and chills, walking as fast as she can. Still I try to cover up, not show any concern. But already Angel is saying her stomach hurts and she doesn't want ice cream, and could we just go straight home.

We walk down the sand, over the path by the bushes of magenta and white beach roses, and along the gravel road to our car. We get the beach bags into the back seat, we get ourselves into the front seats, we get her buckled, we get me buckled, we get the key in the ignition, and we get me looking over my left shoulder to see if it's clear to pull into the road. And there is the man from the beach— black jacket, red face, on a ferocious motorcycle—screaming through my open window. Violence incarnate, he revs his engine, sending grenades straight into our chests, deep into the muscles and right through the bones. His voice is louder even than his engine, though we can't hear a word he says. All we can hear is his rage, which has followed us down the beach and into our car, and, when I am finally able to pull out into the road and onto the shoreline highway, has infiltrated our very bloodstreams.

"Are you sure you don't want ice cream?" I ask the

Angel, but all she wants is to know, "Is he following us?" and "Are you scared?" To both questions I lie and say, "No," though the truth is I'm more angry than scared— angry at this man for stealing my Angel and angry at every man who steals an angel, and angry at myself for making it even more distressing than it had to be.

In my own youth, after I got into the car—white, maybe, big, American—with the man on the corner of 16th and Sanchez, I continued to be approached by other men, with and without cars. But by then I'd learned to recognize and accept and pretend to ignore when men were looking at me the wrong way. There was the time, when we were living at State's student housing, when another scrappy blonde tom girl and I hopped the fence to sneak into a daycare center's playground. I was eleven or twelve, and she was a year younger than me. Her mother had died, so she lived with her father, who had lots of girlfriends, and her older brother, one of those boys who stole cars. Suddenly a man appeared, walking toward us from the closed gate of the playground, smiling too much and talking too softly. Like cats, our ears went up and back, but it wasn't until I was lying on my back, swinging on the rope net, that I knew we were in danger. The man was standing so that every time I swung toward him I bumped into his crotch. When I saw where I was hitting him, and the bulge forming there, I jumped out, grabbed my friend and ran for the fence, wooden, slatted, tall. Footsteps on our tail, we climbed over that fence and raced through the parking garage and back to the crescent of converted army barracks that we called home.

The kids in Gatorville had long talked of the "VD Man," who, in another time or place, would have been called the "Boogie Man." We had no idea what VD was; we just knew it had something to do with sex. And, since we lived on the edge of a college campus in a city that spawned the SLA, Patty Hearst, and serial killers like the Zodiac, there was always some rumor of rapists hiding in the bushes. When we told the kids back home the story of the man in the playground, they wondered if we had, in fact, encountered the VD Man, though I always doubted it since our man was young and clean compared with the picture in my mind of an old, hairy man with the oozing sores of a leper.

To men who leer, and worse, a girl alone at the beach is a girl asking for it. As I grew older—fourteen, seventeen, twenty—and became more of a loner, I was often that girl, in a bikini, working on my tan while reading a novel or doing homework or writing in my journal. By then, I had the full senses of a cat: I could feel trouble before it came into view. I could tell without looking up if someone was lurking in the dunes or lingering too long by the dark-green cedar trees hunched over and stunted from the wind. Sometimes these men just wanted to masturbate to me from a distance. Other times they approached as if invited, though I had given them no such look, and they squatted by my towel or sat on the log I was leaning against and I endured their small talk, keeping my eyes lowered to my book and arms folded across my chest and my answers to their questions curt and cold. Eventually

I learned to look them in the face and smile politely but firmly and say, as if I were a store clerk telling them we were out of their size, "I'm sorry, but I'm not in the mood to talk to anyone. Would you mind leaving me alone?" And they were usually so stunned by my directness that they just left, more in surprise than in anger. Sometimes they even apologized for the "misunderstanding."

One time in Sausalito—I had biked my red Huffy ten-speed up and down and around the hills of San Francisco, over the Golden Gate Bridge, and down into the touristy village tucked between hills and bay—I took my towel out of my backpack and spread it on the ground in a little park to eat lunch and take in the sun. A man in a business suit sat down on the bench too close to my towel. It is things like proximity and duration and speed that tip you off. He gets too close; he stares too long; he walks too slowly. Then there are the gestures—the arms swinging too loosely, the head turning back and forth too frequently, scanning the view but not taking it in. Often he's wearing the wrong clothes, like long pants and shoes at the beach, or an overcoat inside the library. Usually his hands are free; and a person who carries nothing is hoping to run into something instead.

This Marin man threw me a bit. His suit made him seem legit. Plus, I was older—seventeen, about to graduate high school—and eager to start trusting men despite all that I knew about them. Perhaps even businessmen have feelings, and he, like me, had come to this little seaside park to feel the breeze and smell the salt and maybe work out some trouble in his mind. But he sat down too close to me on the bench, and sure enough he started telling me how pretty I was and wondering where I lived and if I wanted to go somewhere with him. When I told him politely that I didn't want to talk, and could he please leave me alone, he politely agreed, though he didn't move on right away. When he finally did leave, he got up slowly, made a point to say goodbye, and ambled away at his own sweet pace.

It wasn't till I got home that night, till I had biked around Sausalito, treated myself to a nonfat peach frozen yogurt then waited in line for the ferry with all the under-dressed shivering tourists, rolled the bike onto the boat and stood with it on the deck as we headed for the fog; it wasn't till I then got off the boat at the foot of Market Street and pedaled all the way up Market to 14th, then up 14th to our apartment, unlocked the black gate, carried the bike up the steps and then wheeled it down our hall and out the kitchen door to the little alley with the gar-bage cans where I locked it up; it wasn't until, exhausted, showered, getting ready for reading in bed, talking with my mother from bathroom to bedroom doorways; it wasn't until I emptied my backpack, dumped out the sand and orange peels, the pen and paper and towel, that I found the note the man had written. It told me every-thing he wanted to say and do to me, which parts of my body he wanted to touch with which parts of his body, and for how long and with what effect.

A decade later, I was walking—quickly, to ward off dan-ger—to my father's studio apartment in a neighborhood made up of warehouses and canneries and artist's lofts. It was dark, deserted, except for one other person, a man, walking right toward me. To avoid him, I crossed the street at an angle. As I reached the other side, the street light went out, and the man shouted something at me. Well-covered in armor, I ignored both the man and the light, and continued on without breaking my stride. The man yelled again, and this time I could hear that the color of his voice was compassion. "Don't get old before you get loved," he said.

But I did not heed his sound advice. Instead, I aged before I ripened. I locked up my youth and beauty, then spent it mostly on men who couldn't love me or who I could not love. It was a long time of keeping my legs closed and my hands to myself before I discovered the liberation of giving in and going after and getting, getting, getting; before sex became for me like water, one of the few things I could immerse myself in, and while in it forget everything except the sensation of being fully alive. Eventually I would learn not just about sex but also about love, but I could never quite see how the two things went together. That equation was one more law of the universe that did not apply to me.

I'm not sure why I remained single as my friends settled down with careers, houses, and husbands, except that those three things seemed wrapped up together in the same package, a package I could not open—partly because I did not know how to open it, and partly because I did not want to. The men I dated were the kind who kept their distance, and I sometimes pitied myself for it. But I was keeping myself from them as well. In the end, yearning and dreaming were my most familiar states of mind, and I remained loyal to them above all else, even love.

Unlike me, my little Angel became a teenager and then a young woman who could dip into pleasure and open herself up to affection. And though we remained friends as she matured, I confess that I adored her most as an eight-year-old, that I adore all girls at that age, when they use their bodies for running, skipping, leaping, bouncing, diving, floating, and soaring. In one photo I have of her, Angel wears a wide grin, her teeth almost too big for her mouth, and an orange tiger lily behind her ear. She is preserved here in the moment of her full potential, with the whole wide world open and possible. I, too, must have once looked, and felt, like that.

After a couple years in Maine, I got a job as an editor at a magazine located in an even more isolated and picturesque town several hours further up the coast. This town was famous for its traditional wooden boatbuilding, and my job provided me with a sailing class as well as access to a fleet of the sweetest and shapeliest wooden boats that anyone could imagine. All I had to do was drop the names of these boats—the Whitehall, the Haven Twelve-and-a-Half, the Cape Cod Catboat—and members of the best New England sailing families would gaze at me with reverence, as if I were the one with the coveted life. Indeed, on the outside, many things about my life seemed splendid: I had bought a surfboard and was spending the warm seasons learning how to catch waves standing up. When not at the beach, I sat with my newest older, detached man on the rustic decadence of his riverside cabin's porch, drinking red wine and watching the tide move the water up and down, in and out, two times a day, every day. He was a happy-go-lucky man known for his wit and independence as well as his red wine, and we spent our time together laughing, dancing, drinking, cooking, and making love, never mentioning the future or anything else potentially serious. So for a little while at least, I could feel happy go lucky, too.

One warm afternoon, I was sitting on the dock in the boatyard with a friend from work. We were talking about a dream I kept having in which I would save children from drowning. I was in my mid-thirties, and had been having the dream for years, in daytime and nighttime, in various incarnations, including apocalyptic waves on sloping seashores and muddy Hudson River dives off rickety piers. It was my version of Holden Caulfield and his catcher in the rye. Like Holden, I wanted to save all children before they fell into life's miasma of pain and sex and broken hearts, that great and awful sea of joy and loneliness. I wanted to keep them safely in their eight-year-old bliss, protected from despair and away from men and ambition and infinity—things that had given me such trouble.

A little girl, blonde, missing teeth, sat a few feet from us on the dock's edge. To dangle her feet in the water, she had to stretch quite far out and down, so not much of her was actually sitting on the weathered wood surface. We talked about the boats she'd been on and the ones she wanted to go on, and how she didn't like the little ones because they were tippy. The way she was leaning, like an arrow pointed down, set her body a little off balance, so if she were to lose her grip, she would slip right into the cold, green water. But I didn't say this to her because I didn't want her to feel fearful, and because she was just three feet away from me, and I knew I could yank her out if she did fall in. Then her mother called from the boathouse and she went running.

A few days later I got word that a drowning had happened, not to the little girl, not, in fact, to anyone I'd ever met. It happened at the pond on the farm where I used to live, the pond I had once canoed with Angel on a Saturday in summer. A young man of twenty, young enough to be called a child, was visiting someone in the area. He was from out of state; he couldn't swim. I didn't know the details—how deep, how long—but I knew that pond well, having swum there in the wee hours of nights ending and days beginning, in bleached hot afternoons with children shouting, and, in winter, having glided around its surface on thin metal blades. I knew that water, murky brown, almost red, impossible to see through. It was warm on the surface, but as you approached the bottom and the stream that fed it, the dark cold could overwhelm.

The boy, or the man, was not dead yet. He was hooked up to machines in the hospital, machines that didn't register a mark when reading his brain. His parents traveled up from Massachusetts to talk to doctors and make decisions. I imagined them pale, shaking, looking down at their son under the fluorescent lights and wondering what to do with him. It was a Sunday when the boy went under, when the sounds and colors of panic were striking, when a body was forgetting how to hold air. At the beach just three miles away, I was immersed in water myself—gleefully, gratefully, the waves pushing and pulling me. I was under their arches and inside their curves, holding my breath against their crashes, and surfacing into a face full of foam. My skin alert and salty, my eyes open and then closed, I was on top of those waves, riding them like you would ride a wild horse.

I don't understand how a body floats, or how it sinks. I don't understand how things go from clear to dirty to pure again, or how I became one of the lucky ones and made it to the other side. I simply fell into that great and awful sea, and started thrashing my arms and legs, elbows and ankles, till somehow survival turned into ecstasy and for a moment, at least, everything, *everything*, seemed promising. I was not able to save that boy, or to save my little Angel, either. But suddenly, finally, I felt able to save myself. I wasn't sure how, but I could see, for the first time, that it was possible.

CHAPTER 15
GO FLY A KITE

I was on a trip back "home" to Northern California—part work, part vacation—and I had a terrible head cold. My research for a magazine article on the food and wine of the counties north of San Francisco had brought me to a chilly town on the edge of the San Andreas Fault, a town populated by a combination of high-end tourists, ranch hands, and hippie holdouts. There, alongside the gift shops, feed store, and yoga studio, I stumbled across an herbal apothecary with a hand-painted sign that said "Garden of Eden." I stepped into this garden to buy some echinacea to supplement the Sudafed and Tylenol I was already taking (when feeling this low, I discriminated against no potential cure). The shopkeeper, whose long, graying brown hair identified her as one of the holdouts, watched me peruse her shelves, then asked, in a surprising French accent, what my symptoms were.

"If you like," she said, "I can mix up a custom tincture for your problems."

She grew or collected all the herbs herself, and she seemed to know what she was doing with them, so I offered up my symptoms to her: sore throat, congestion, headache, fatigue. With that, she turned to her work-bench, a two-tiered table covered with large bottles of various mud-colored extracts, and began to pour. But my problems didn't end with my cold symptoms.

"Oh, yeah," I said to the hair spilling down her back, "and my love life is a shambles, and I lose interest in any-thing I pursue, and I don't know where to call home. You got anything for that?"

Eden—it turns out that was her name on the sign, not the name her mother had given her, but the name she had given herself—approached me with a handful of colored paper and asked me to choose one for the label. And as she wrote out the directions ("half a dropper three times a day, with prayer") on the saffron paper I'd selected, she told me that she was studying Sufism.

"The Sufis are the ones who do the dancing?" I asked. It was all I knew about Sufis. Once, when revisiting the houses and apartments in San Francisco where I'd lived as a child, I'd encountered a Sufi commune, whirling like the dervishes they were. They'd moved into the house on Norwich Street where my first memories took place—eating a parsley sandwich from a floating pie pan in the bathtub, slamming the window on my finger, reminding my older brother in the middle of the night to turn the pillow over to the cool side.

"Sufi is the mystical form of Islam," Eden explained. "In a healing we don't dance; we breathe and chant and pray to Allah—though if you're not comfortable using that word you can pray to whoever you want." Then she offered to give me a free healing; she was in the student-teaching phase of her program and needed to practice. "The healing could address some of those other concerns you mentioned," she said with a little smile.

"I'm not really religious," I explained to her. "I'm not even what you would call spiritual." I gave her a brief run-down of how my parents—one Catholic, one Jewish—had abandoned their religions at a young age, and didn't have time to figure out what to tell their children before we started popping out, one, two, three of us, curious, impressionable, and eager for stories that might help us live out our lives. "But they did manage to teach us awe and humility," I told Eden, "so I've never had the gall to disbelieve in the possibility that something benevolent or at least concerned might be trying to orchestrate behind the scenes."

If pressed, I'd have to call myself an agnostic—an I-don't-knower—who doesn't quite discount magic, luck, or coincidence, either; someone who, just in case, picks pennies off the ground if they're facing up, and makes wishes on stars, moons, planets, and anything else that twinkles in the night sky. What I don't believe in are con-gregations. As a child, I watched teenagers, grown-ups, and whole families join the Hare Krishnas, Scientology, Lifespring, Synanon, the Moonies, and various other groups that liked to accost you with free personality tests or spice-dusted popcorn as you walked along Mar-ket or Mission Street. An imperviousness to cults, clans, and clubs is a blessing when one waits for you on every street corner, hoping to catch you in the aftermath of a fight with your lover or your mother or your boss—or other times when you might be particularly susceptible to kindness. But my skin was perhaps unnecessarily tough, sealing me off from strangers but also from strange-sounding things—reiki, shiatsu, Feldenkrais—that may have been able to do me some good. I came of age in the center of the New Age—in both time and place—and was currently an editor at a magazine called *New Age*, which required me to take seriously all kinds of theories and practices I didn't believe in. Through it all my resistance had remained firm. But that day in Eden's shop, something in me melted just a bit. It was time, I supposed, to cast off at least a piece of the armor I'd been wearing for decades. Plus it was free.

"Okay," I told her, through the haze of my head cold. "I'll give it a try." We arranged a healing session for the following week, on a day that, as coincidence or God or the stars would have it, happened to be my thirty-ninth birthday.

In other parts of the country, February is dreary and cold, a time of bare branches against a gray sky, but in Northern California it is a month of pink and white blossoms emerging from moist, vibrant green. It wasn't until my first semester at the New England college that I understood what my high school English teachers had meant when they'd said winter is a symbol for death. In California, things die in summer, when the rains stop and the heat bleaches the grass to a pale, crispy brown. Winter, by contrast, is the season when water pumps life into rivers and fields, creating rich black soils covered with improbable shades of green. After twenty-something years on the East Coast, I was back for an extended visit during the month of February, and I almost couldn't adjust to the lush vitality humming all around me. As with dozens of trips I'd made back to California over the years, I spent much of my time trying to convince myself that I had every right to partake in such beauty and opulence.

In New England, people would ask me why I'd ever left San Francisco, that city of light and charm. But for me, San Francisco is the place where I became a Have Not; a city of sadness and divorce and impossible dreams; a city drenched in cold, damp fog, while just over the bridge— any bridge—the sun is shining and anything is possible. So I stayed away for decades, afraid that whatever fragile sense of possibility I had created would not be able to survive a return to my birthplace. Finally, however, I had done everything I wanted to do on the East Coast. The small town in Maine had become too cozy, and I missed this northwestern landscape: the soft, sloping hills going down to the Pacific, the foggy wind that whipped through the valleys, the green-and-cream streetcars and bright gray sidewalks of the city. This was the geography imprinted upon me at my most impressionable age, and I had begun yearning to see it again. I also had young nieces now, the children of my younger brother, and I wanted to take advantage of this chance to be part, once again, of a family.

But as soon as I'd stepped off the plane and into San Francisco, city of my original disappointment, the wavering had begun. No one was there to pick me up—it just wasn't done in our family—and on the bus from the airport, I'd closed my eyes against the city and even the bridge, not opening them until we'd passed into Marin county, then Sonoma, where both my father and younger brother had settled. Neither father nor brother met me at the bus stop, so I took a five-dollar taxi ride to my brother's house, where he lived with his wife and two girls. And with this hollow thud, I was "home," trying with all my might to remind myself of my right, and my desire, to be here.

On the morning of my birthday, Eden and I sat in her little shop with the door locked and the CLOSED sign in the window. The sun was out and the sky was clear, but the damp chill of the ocean air seeped under the door and through the threads of our sweaters. She had asked me to come up with a concern—physical or emotional—that I wanted to work on, and so once again I was confronted with the question *What seems to be the problem?* Though I'd been having on-and-off pain in the lower back for some years and a lifetime of insomnia and digestive problems, I wanted to focus on the one problem that felt most impossible to solve. I'd spent the week tracing my ailments back to their origins, trying to describe this mother of all problems, the Big Kahuna from which all the others hatched. It's hard to condense a life's worth of trouble into words, and once you've done it, those troubles can come off sounding petty.

They refer to poor kids these days as "at risk," but

when I was a child, the word was "deprived," and there was something accurate, if condescending, about the concept of deprivation. I grew up wanting many things, including a safe and reliable home where the family ate dinner together every night and the kids had to call to ask permission to miss a meal or arrive late. But even after I got out from under the laws and habits and necessities of poverty that my family had lived by, even after I got jobs and apartments and stereos, I still couldn't shake the sense of scarcity. I no longer *had* to live in poverty and want, but I chose to dwell there nonetheless because I knew no other way to live.

"My problem is in my head," I told Eden, who regarded me with a serene, closed-mouth smile. "Or at least that's where it started, but then it spread out to every part of my body, like a cancer. It's not actually a thing. It's an idea, or a belief, really. In fact, it's a lie. But it *feels* so real that it might as well be a physical disease."

"And what is the belief?" Eden asked.

"That things that are possible for other people are not possible for me. That I am excluded." *Honestly*, I thought to myself, *haven't I gotten rid of this ridiculous theory yet?* After all these years, I was bored of my own way of seeing the world, and in so many ways the evidence no longer supported it. Back East, I had a decent car and a good job with health insurance and a retirement account. I owned a small sailboat and a long surfboard and made use of both. I'd spent my summer vacation in France— flying into Paris to rendezvous with a man I'd only dated twice before, then surfing the beaches down the Atlantic

coast to Biarritz. The article I was currently working on—
about the vineyards, restaurants, and spas of the wine
country—would go on to earn me a nomination for a
prestigious James Beard Award for food writing, bringing
me to an Oscar-like gala in New York City filled with the
world's top food celebrities. But this other version of me
still felt tenuous, and I didn't know how to hold onto my
new self in my old setting.

"Excluded from what?" Eden asked, her tone somewhere between compassion and incredulity. Sometimes I
forgot that I looked normal on the outside, and that the
"exclusion principle" I'd invented in junior high school
could be invisible to others, no matter how pervasive it
felt to me.

"Everything," I said, trying to convey how deep this
belief went. "A husband. A home. Nice underwear. Dinner parties with stimulating conversation. Vacations
abroad. A garden with nasturtiums and sunflowers…" As
I was listing these things, I realized that I'd actually *had*
some of them, but, curiously, that didn't stop them from
feeling like they were out of my reach. I always chose the
off-brand, on-sale, low-cost version; either that or I got a
scholarship, a pity gift, or stole the thing. So even when
I got a hold of the car, the surfboard, the boyfriend, the
vacation, it felt cheapened, and I went on yearning. In my
hands, possessions and accomplishments felt insubstan-
tial, as elusive as smoke.

In reflexology, it's the feet, in chiropractic, it's the spine,
and in Sufism, it's the heart that acts as a template for

what's going on with the rest of you. Touching her hand to her chest, Eden explained that Sufis believe the space surrounding your heart contains connections to every other part of your body and mind. We closed our eyes and breathed deeply for a few minutes. Then she asked me how my heart felt. Over the next hour and a half she would return to that question again and again, forcing me delicately—like a pediatrician with a nervous child—to pay attention to my feelings in a way that I had never done before. "It hurts a little," was my first response. "It feels kind of tight."

In my previous outings with helping professionals—ones with degrees and licenses—I'd been asked many times how I felt about this or that. "And how does that make you feel?" they'd say, especially when I was trying to get *their* opinion on something. "Angry," I might respond, or "disappointed." It was always an emotional feeling they were after. But when Eden asked me how I felt, she was inquiring into my *physical* condition. "Sore," I said, my palm on my chest between my breasts, "a bit warm." Talk therapy had helped me to identify and articulate problems and even come up with explanations and solutions for them, but how do you turn an explanation into a belief? How does your mind convince your body, your whole self, to follow its logic? How do you get an idea—however good or right it may be—to penetrate all the way down through skin and muscle, into the marrow of the bones, the place where blood is made and then sent out to all the organs? Perhaps this Sufi emphasis on physical sensation would do what years of mental fretting and figuring could not.

We breathed deeply while Eden talked me through a series of visualizations. First she wanted me to imagine my connection to the core of the earth, to think of my tailbone stretching into the trunk of a tree, or of a strong rope with an anchor grounding me all the way down to the solid heart of the planet.

The tree image didn't work for me, so I tried several ropes, mostly nautical, including a thick, worn hemp line and a silky white braid. But I couldn't find one that would take me all the way down into the core of the earth. It was too late, anyway; we were moving on. It was time to reach up like the branches of a tree to the infinite sky, to open up to the light and the heavens. I had no more luck going above than I did below: my imagination was held captive by my cynicism.

Now we began to chant. It wasn't a rhythmic chant. We had one word, *Allah*, and we said it in many different ways: sometimes in rapid succession, sometimes drawing out the two lush syllables, rolling them around in our mouths before exhaling them in long, slow breaths. We said this buttery word over and over for a few minutes straight, and then we came back to it like to a rest stop throughout the session whenever we got distracted or overwhelmed.

"Now tell me about your problem," Eden said. "Where do you feel it?"

"Right here," I said, and surprised myself by pointing to my lower back. Until that moment, I'd thought it was in my head.

"What does it feel like?" she asked.

"Like something is tied to me there," I said, aware suddenly of a tugging at my lower back restraining me. I could shake my torso and wave my arms and legs, but all that movement would get me nowhere, because my sacrum—the part of the body that the Ancient Greeks called the "holy bone"—was being pulled back and down, fastening me to the ground.

"What's tying you down?" Eden asked, in her French pediatrician's voice.

And now an image came to me, to my body and my mind at the same time, so that I both saw and felt it. It wasn't, as Eden had suggested, rope or chain tying me down. It was something seemingly benign: kite string. Hundreds of pieces of thin white kite string were attached to the small of my back—the very spot that had been giving me chronic, sometimes acute pain ever since I'd fallen down a flight of stairs seven or eight years earlier. Kite string may be lightweight, but I knew, from an illustrated version of *Gulliver's Travels* that we'd had at the flat on 16th and Sanchez, that enough of it could keep someone immobilized. And this kite string had something on it that magnified its power: each strand was coated in glass, like the strings of the Korean fighting kites I'd seen as a child, lunging at each other in the mighty wind of San Francisco's marina. Those kites, manipulated by calm, masterful men standing on the grassy field there, would literally cut each other off at the string, sending the losing kite out to sea. Back in the schoolyard of our neighborhood, my brothers and I would try to make our own kites with sticks and rags and the cardboard tubes from rolls of toilet paper. Then, if we could get them aloft, we'd try to get them to fight.

Eden and I took some more deep breaths, bringing our word, *Allah*, in and out, rolling it over the teeth and the tongue, gargling with it in the throat. We spent many minutes with this image of the kite strings, feeling the tightness, the pain and frustration of trying to move forward and up, but being able only to wriggle sideways, with limbs flailing, like a beetle on its back. Then Eden asked, "What would it feel like if you didn't have the strings pulling you down?"

Ping. Ping, ping, ping. As soon as she said this, they started popping one by one, thin coatings of glass shattering in tiny showers, like miniature fireworks. With each *ping* I felt lighter, until I was rising up, just like a kite should. Soon all the strings had snapped, and I was flying fast and high, but not so high that I could be carried away. A long piece of fabric, like the tails for our schoolyard kites, tethered me loosely but securely to someone or something on the ground, so I could swoop and soar in the wind but not have to worry about getting carried away. I was like a dog with the longest, softest leash in the world, free but safe, connected to some masterful presence on the ground who was both kind and in command.

Allah. Aaaaallah, we said. Then from high above, where I was flying like a kite, I looked down to see the rough brown sands of a Northern California beach. The beaches in this half of the state are not brimming with bikinis, surfboards, and volleyballs. Most of the year—especially

summer, when the coast is filled with fog and wind—
you're more likely to be wearing long pants and a sweatshirt than a bathing suit. But these harsh, pigeon-colored
sands are the beaches of my childhood, and I have fond
memories of salty logs burning into orange embers in a
driftwood fire, of the pounding then the *shhhhh* of the
waves hitting the sand and receding, of making sand
angels with my brothers. As I looked down at those
beaches from above Eden's garden, my body remembered
how it had felt on those family outings, when excitement
and safety and adventure and belonging were all in perfect balance. All of my wants were fulfilled, and I could,
without thinking about it, lean into the world and rely
on it to support me. Regardless of the mistakes and accidents involved, the members of my family had belonged
together. This was the time of my great wealth, when I
had everything I needed—hot dogs, campfires, brothers,
parents—and it was enough.

"Now, Frances," Eden said, in the gentle voice of a
nurse waking a patient, "I want you to ask God what he
wants to make for you."

It wasn't quite clear to me why Eden used the word
make. Maybe there was some ambiguity in French, as
there is in Spanish, between the verbs "to make" and "to
do." But I didn't want to break out of my reveries to ask
for a clarification, nor to remind her that I didn't necessarily believe in God. For an I-don't-knower, to invoke
God, or Allah, is to invoke Hope. It is to hope that you
don't understand everything, that there is something or
someone out there who might be in charge, like that giant

chess player in the sky I imagined when I was little and just discovering the infiniteness of the universe. It is to hope that something you cannot see or smell or touch is not just able but willing to help you out, to reach down and reposition the bishops, the knights, the pawns, creating a little escape route for you. "God?" I said tentatively, "what do you want for me?"

"Ask him what he wants to *give* you," nudged Eden.

I did, and as soon as the words left my mouth I heard God laughing. It was a giggle, kind of feminine, not at all cruel. I didn't so much hear it as feel it in my body. This creature—a skinny little dark guy like Gandhi, who went by the name of "God"—was laughing at me for asking such a ridiculous question, and I, too, began to laugh.

"What is he saying?" Eden wanted to know.

"He's laughing," I told her. "He's saying, 'What do I want to give you? Silly girl, I've already given it to you.'"

And indeed he had, thirty-nine years ago to the day. He, she, it; love, lust, luck; magic, biology, evolution, or accident—or perhaps some combination of all these and more had gotten together and given me a life. My mission was simply to flesh out the story; to inhabit it to my true potential, to stop wanting and start being.

Holey Moley, I thought, in my cold, damp state of enlightenment. *Have I gone cultish at last?*

Had I finally become infected by all the perky self-help and vaguely Eastern books I'd had to review for the magazine? Was I having what people I consider flakes might call a "spiritual moment"? Did I believe suddenly that my poverty was just a figment of my imagination?

That all along, I'd actually been rich and "blessed" (whatever the hell that means) but had simply never realized it? Was I becoming one of those pseudo-Buddhist California prospertarians who can't open their mouths without the word *abundance* dropping out? Who say that world hunger is just a state of mind, and if we all stopped believing in it, it would cease to be? Who subscribe to the philosophy that you can get everything you want—including cash, a winning touchdown, and an exciting yet reliable husband—by simply imagining you already have it and being grateful? Who declare that "there are no accidents," that "everything happens for a reason" and that all you have to do in life is "put it out there and the universe will provide"?

No, I had not converted to positive thinking, and was still relatively safe from the dangers of enlightenment. In fact, as I hugged Eden goodbye and walked out of her garden, I was feeling as pragmatic as ever. I had simply begun to realize, through low-level hypnosis or guided meditation or whatever this Sufi healing really was, that it was a pitiful waste to spend my days and nights on this very solid earth wallowing in the misty elusiveness of want; that there is no white hot circle of fame or love or plenty where everything is finally perfect; that people always desire things they don't have; that every girl has her story, and though often it is not the one she wishes for, it is her story nonetheless.

From the shop, I drove out to a trailhead on a nearby ridge. A notorious fire had blasted through these hills a decade earlier, and all around the charred trees loomed.

The smell of ash was long gone, however, replaced by an invigorating sage aroma from the wild shrubs that cover these coastal slopes, and by a sea-salt musk rising up from the ocean somewhere below me, just out of my sight. "There are ninety-nine names for Allah, but only one god," Eden had told me, and the name she'd seen streaming into my heart like a shaft of light was number eighteen: *Allah al Fattah*, the Opener. At the end of our session, we'd looked up al Fattah in one of her books: "When we find ourselves confronted with a totally new view of ourselves," she'd read, "we may have to take a leap of faith into the unknown, which can feel like annihilation." But al Fattah had appeared to help me open up to my new self, Eden had declared, and I could call on him by saying his name aloud sixty times.

So as I walked up the slope of the trail, I said his name over and over, trying to get to sixty. I said his name out to the thriving new pines and to the bare, blackened trunks alike. "Allah al Fattah," I said, calling on this thing that I did not believe in but nonetheless hoped would help me annihilate—oh, what a tantalizing idea—my old self. The idea that I might be able to open up to this world, and the world to me, made me giddy. Hiding behind that giddiness, however, was a slim pessimism, readying itself for the crash. Would this spell soon wear off, or would my new attitude be the one that would finally settle in and take root?

Life is not a book. It doesn't get divided into sixteen neat chapters with a mounting conflict, epiphany, and resolution. Instead, we take a step backward for every one we take forward, and often what we think is an epiphany turns out to be a fleeting moment of inanity. I'd had great realizations before, instances of clarity when I could see that the world was neither for nor against me. And little by little I'd inched forward—or sideways, like a crab, looking back while moving on a diagonal. By now I understood that my problems were both inside and outside me, that psychology and economics, vision and belief all played a role; that the world was unfair, but not unworkable. Many people had it worse than me, and some had it better, but in the end I could get most of what I really wanted. My parents had not had the means to give me the things that money, or even nurture, can buy. But they had given me curiosity, and compassion, and creativity—and what could not be constructed out of these? My mother, pulling herself up and out of so many difficulties, had taught me that it was possible to survive anything, including despair. My father, by giving me so much rope, had taught me to tie knots and rescue myself. And they had both passed on to me their ability to spot the absurdities in the world and laugh out loud at the.

The trail led me to a clearing on the western face of the ridge. The ocean was somewhere out there in front of me, but a thick layer of fog concealed it. "Allah al Fattah," I said, turning back to the trail, matching my words to my footsteps, my footsteps to my breath.

Chapter 16
Become Your Own Enemy

A couple years later, after two decades on the East Coast, I moved back west, hoping that I might finally be ready to reach up and pluck a few of those mythical California oranges of my own. I'd quit my magazine job to go free-lance, and had enough money in the bank to infuse me with a thin stream of enthusiasm about my return to the land of plenty. My first stop was the guest room of my younger brother's Sonoma County house, where I spent several months basking in, though not quite belonging to, the home life he'd somehow created: wife, children, pets. This little box of a room, in a neighborhood with slim driveways and miniature lawns, was the only spare room available in my family. Though my father had built a sweet cabin in a remote redwood canyon further north, it remained rough and unfinished and too far away; it was a good place to spend a day or two, sleeping on a futon couch in the living room, walking through my father's bedroom to get to the bathroom. Over the years I had often ended up there, especially when recovering from a break-up or a break-down, grateful for my father's detachment, which allowed me to just eat, read, and sleep. My mother and older brother, who each lived alone in the city, also had couches, or at least space on the floor for a sleeping bag, but no place for me to settle in while I figured out where to settle down.

At my going-away party back east, the staff at the magazine wished me well and handed me an envelope to help me on my way. My colleagues had heard me talk about how the pounding Pacific waves required a surfboard very different from the one I used on the gentler Maine surf, so they'd taken up a collection and bought me a gift certificate from a surf shop close to my brother's house. With a couple hundred dollars added from me, it would buy me a board to start me off right on my new West Coast life. If my friends from work had known about my history with gift certificates, how hard it was for me to spend money—or its facsimile—on myself, they would have bought a board for me. But when I stepped into that shop, just across town from my younger brother's house, the onus was on me.

Oh, the boards in that store were luscious, their long, voluptuous curves glistening in the golden light diffused through the windows. The finishes were smooth and shiny, unblemished, unscratched, almost untouchable. The dimensions on those boards—their length, width, and thickness, how much curve they had at the nose, how pointed they got at the tail—were created with the Northern California waves in mind. They were lightweight but heavy-duty. They were extra buoyant and easy to paddle. They were just what I needed, and I went in there three, four, five times, salivating.

But of course, I didn't buy one of those new, perfect surfboards. I bought a used board through a classified ad for a lot cheaper. It had some scratches and yellow spots where it was taking on water. It was poorly shaped and hard to paddle, even harder to maneuver. The gift certificate I spent over the next year or two, on accessories—a neoprene cap, a surfboard cover, a plastic board protector I never even opened—asking the owner to deduct small amounts from my gift certificate each time. Eventually the shop changed hands, and the final twenty bucks on my certificate just disappeared. Obviously, I still had a lot to learn about getting and spending.

After living at my younger brother's house for six months, I took my laptop and my new used longboard and spent a month in a seaside village in Mexico. A friend, who I'd met while traveling the year earlier, had invited me to stay at her vacation home, Casa del Sol, located a few blocks from the beach. I figured I might as well work on my freelance assignments in a place where I could walk around in a sarong and flip-flops and practice my Spanish as well as my surfing. It sounded like paradise, like a life that someone else should be living and I should only be hearing about.

My first morning in Paradise, my hostess woke me up with the news that the house had been broken into during the night.

"They left our packs out on the terrace in a little pile," she said, standing in the blare of the sunlight outside my room. I was so groggy I didn't quite get what this meant, or how it affected me. I started to get up to look—maybe a visual would make the information concrete—then remembered to check the six-inch crack between the head of the bed and the wall, where I'd stashed my laptop in its padded case: Gone. Now I was awake. That laptop had my articles and stories on it; it was my life and my livelihood. I jumped out of bed, pulled on some shorts, and joined my hostess and her other guest on the wide catwalk outside the three bedrooms.

They had been very polite thieves. They'd gone into each of our rooms, carried our bags out to the porch, removed the valuables, and left the rest in a neat pile, so we'd still have clothes to wear and books to read and lotion to rub on our skin. They'd left behind—or perhaps they'd missed—our passports, airplane tickets, and credit cards, which we'd stashed in particularly good spots. They had also been very daring thieves, searching through the pockets of the clothes my hostess had thrown on the back of her chair, opening the nightstand drawer where her other guest had put his watch, and reaching within inches of my head, which was resting on a pillow, to extract my computer from its hiding place. This image, of a stranger entering the room while I slept and leaning down close enough to kiss me—and who knows, maybe he did—would haunt me for weeks. How did the thief, or thieves, know we would not wake up? What would have happened if I *had* woken up to the sight of a man, let's just presume it was a man, hovering so close to my sleeping body?

My first thought, as I bent down to that pile of our discarded possessions on the terrace, was disbelief: *This is not really happening.* My hostess stood above me, her short dark hair hitting her chin, emphasizing her mouth, which was set into a cynical frown. She had no trouble believing in the facts. Neither did the other guest, who was just visiting for a few days, and who was pounding his feet on the tile floor and swearing at those absent thieves.

My second thought was, like his, directed at the robbers: *How could they do this to me; I'm one of them.* I, too, was a poor kid from a place buckling under the pressures of tourism and gentrification; I, too, watched rich people from elsewhere move into my town, my neighborhood— into my house, in the case of my childhood flat on 16th Street—and then get ripped off because they were dumb enough to leave their windows open or their shiny new cars parked on our dangerous streets. But of course, in this small Mexican village on a placid Pacific beach, I wasn't one of them. Here, I was a *gringa* from elsewhere, rich enough to own a laptop and stupid enough to get it stolen. I may have sneered at the Americans surfing in their skimpy swimsuits while the locals worked for *pesos*, but I was a skimpy-suit-wearing surfer myself. That's one of the downsides of upward mobility: You eventually become the people you once resented.

Still, I was determined to get my computer, and my pride, back. That morning, the other guest and I found a few of our things, including my bulky Nikon camera, in the brush around the house, as if the robbers had found them too heavy and tossed them on their way out. As the

air got hazy with heat, I spent another hour searching
the bushes on that dry hillside, hoping to find my navy
blue laptop case, and hoping not to find any scorpions or
snakes. Instead, at the top of the hill, I encountered a nine-
year-old boy sitting on a rock, watching me with uncon-
tainable curiosity. When I told him about the break-in,
he leapt off the rock, landed in a squat, then stood up and
put one finger in the air. "*Ladrones*?" he said. "Robbers?"
Then, sounding a lot like the Underdog cartoon, "I'll find
them for you."

Underdog accompanied me back down the hill—
holding his hand out to me so I wouldn't slip on the
crumbling auburn gravel—where I canvassed the neighborhood, ending up at the local market at the bottom of
our road. The proprietress, who smelled of beer, shook
her head slowly and made the "tsk-tsk" sound, though it
wasn't clear if she was "tsking" me for providing the robbers with the opportunity for crime or "tsking" the robbers for taking it.

"*El Muerto*," she said, still shaking her head. It was the
same thing the next-door neighbors had said to me. El
Muerto means "death" or "the dead one," but here it was
the nickname of a local hoodlum, a man known for doing
drugs on the hilltop above the house where I was staying. Each time someone said his name, eyes down, heads
shaking slowly, I imagined a frightening devil of a man
with a pockmarked face and stringy black hair, skinny as
a skeleton from heroin, a kind of evil Keith Richards.

The only local official was a man everyone referred
to as the *juez*, so I tracked him down at the liquor store

he owned on the main street and reported the crime. Juez translates as "judge," but this little man, who served as a kind of liaison to the municipal world outside of the village, seemed to wield about as much power as a notary public. Still, he did have one of the few phones in town, so he called the police for me, then told me to go back to the house and wait for them to drive over from their headquarters several towns to the north. An hour later— this was the only thing that happened fast the whole time I was in Mexico—the juez appeared on the front patio of Casa del Sol with *el Comandante* and his assistant, both dressed in khaki uniforms.

After the assistant got my name, age, and marital status, the Comandante started in on the real questions. "Were the doors locked?" he asked me.

It was not an easy question to answer. In the architectural style of northern gringos who build second homes in warm third-world countries, a style that could be termed "Vacation Naïve," Casa del Sol did not have doors. In fact, it hardly had walls, and not very many ceilings, either. It did have lots of floors, though—thick, tiled, and built on a solid poured-concrete foundation—and in this way it was really the opposite of the homes of all our Mexican neighbors, who put their limited resources into solid cinderblock walls with ceilings and doors (with locks), sometimes leaving the floor raw with dirt. At Casa del Sol, you walked from the drive right onto a terrace, then up a wide staircase to an open kitchen, with a bathroom tucked around a half-wall, out of sight but not out of hearing. A half-roof made of palm fronds covered the cooking area, but otherwise the place was open to the sky. Similarly, the exterior wall covered the back and one side of the house, leaving half the house open to views of the sun (hence the name, Casa del Sol, House of the Sun) and sweet breezes—and also to snakes, dirt, rain, and robbers. Downstairs, the bedrooms were carved like three caves out of the back wall, each facing the wide, tiled walkway, and each fronted with a black iron gate. But, as I explained to the Comandante, my hostess only locked those gates when we left the house. So, no, the doors, such as they were, had not been locked the night before.

The Comandante did not even have to shake his head or make the "tsk-tsk" sound to let me know I was an idiot for carrying a backpack, a surfboard, and a laptop computer case into that house in broad daylight under the watchful eyes of whomever, and not locking the gate behind me when I went to sleep. Now he wanted to know how the robber was able to go into each bedroom, open drawers and zippers, fidget with pockets full of change, without waking up any of us. Frankly, I had the same question. How *did* the robber manage to time his entry so well, avoiding the fitful waking-and-sleeping sessions of our first hot, noisy night in Mexico, watching the lamps in each of our rooms go on and off, as one or the other of us got up to read or make a trip to the bathroom, and waiting precisely until all three of us had settled into a deep and impenetrable REM phase?

Next the Comandante wanted to know if we woke up with headaches. Apparently this officer watched too many black-and-white gangster movies, because he seemed to think someone had slipped us a mickey, then tailed us back to the house to wait until we passed out. When I dissuaded him of that theory, he wondered if it were the thieves that had been on drugs: who would explain their unexplainable behavior, how they could walk so audaciously into our rooms as we slept, why they took my Nikon only to leave it behind on the hillside. When I told him about the neighbors suspecting El Muerto, the Comandante nodded his head with confidence; he knew the name well. "El Muerto," he repeated. "*Drogas.*"

After a few more questions, the Comandante told me he could do nothing further—not even look in the bushes surrounding the house, where the laptop might have been hiding among the boa constrictors—until I filed an *anuncio*, a word he pronounced with the utmost respect, as if it were an article of the church. In order to make this anuncio—it turned out to be a kind of police report—I had to travel by buses to a municipal office located several towns to the south, sign numerous carbon copies, and place my inked thumbprint next to my signature on each copy.

While I waited, and waited, and waited for the Comandante to come back and start the investigation, I did what I could to find the robbers on my own. I befriended every coplike figure in town, from the local security force to the highway patrol guys who just happened to be passing through for lunch. If they wore a uniform—even just a polo shirt with an insignia—I tried to enlist their help. I put up posters and offered a reward. I hounded the juez, visiting every single day to ask if he'd heard from the police. I stopped the buses that drove into and out of town and told the drivers to be on the lookout for someone smuggling out my laptop case. Then one morning, I ran into a local man I'd met through my hostess; he was an artist and a stonemason, and had overseen the construction of Casa del Sol. So when I told him about the break-in, he reacted as if personally affronted. We stood on a dirt street corner in the center of town, and I told him that the robbers had not just taken a machine, but the tool I used to create literature, to express myself, and to earn my living.

One night, just after my parents divorced, my father cashed his paycheck, piled the three kids into the cab of his white International pick-up, and drove out to the malls just south of the city limits. It was four days before Christmas, and we were shopping for sweaters, shoes, basketballs, and everything else that would be wrapped up and stuck under our tree for our first holiday without our dad. After hitting a bunch of stores, piling bags and boxes into the crevice between the seatback and the window, we pulled into the parking lot of one more shopping center. When we returned to the truck an hour later, fully spent, the door was open and all our Christmas presents were gone. We stood in silence, under a tall street light, unable to believe that the world could be so mean.

My father rarely gave us advice or admonitions; he belonged to the "give-em-enough-rope" school of parenting, and felt that mistakes were their own best teachers. But this night, when we were finally able to speak, he tried his best to turn the stolen presents into a lesson.

"You never know how hard you're hitting someone," he said on the drive back home in the empty truck, his voice wet and unsteady with tears. He knew his children coveted things, and therefore sometimes stole them. And he believed in the power of empathy. "That's what I hope you kids remember about this. How hard it can hit you." The next day he borrowed money from a friend and drove around by himself trying to rebuy all the presents we had picked out.

Like my father, I believed in a camaraderie of the downtrodden, and thought that if the robbers who took my laptop knew me, if they understood that I was also just a struggling underdog trying to make her way, they would choose to steal from someone else instead, someone who could afford it, and maybe even deserved it. Standing on the red dirt street corner with the Mexican stonemason, I shared my theory. "If I could explain to those thieves how much I need that computer to eke out my living, maybe they'd return it to me," I told him.

"*Pues, vamos,*" he said; "Well then, let's go." He knew El Muerto and his sidekick Julio, and offered to take me to their houses. It was almost noon and the sun was beating down. My friends and all other sensible vacationers were in the water or the shade. But the stonemason and I walked out into that sun, across the bridge into the side of town where the homes had walls and doors and locks but no names, stopping outside a small, square house. A rudimentary weightlifting bench sat in the front yard, and I imagined El Muerto's physique, bulging with muscles and cruelty. The surroundings might have been humble—the street, like all the streets in this town, was dirt; the paint on the house was dusted with a layer of that pale dry dirt; the doors and windows were open to the flies and the heat—but the process was formal. We did not knock on the door or even approach it; instead we stood in the street in front of the house and announced ourselves. Then a woman, maybe my age, in an apron, came to the door. Two young kids followed her, and they all three stared at us, at me in particular.

"*Buenos dias*," the mom said, her voice apprehensive, so it sounded more like a question than a statement: "Is it a good morning?"

"We're here to see El Muerto," the stonemason told her, and the woman—was she Mrs. El Muerto?—disappeared back into the darkness of the doorway, leaving the two little boys to continue staring. The stonemason and I remained at our respectful distance from the house, not having been invited closer, and after a few minutes the kids grew tired of staring at me and started playing on the weight bench instead. Finally a young man emerged from the doorway with a grin. He was no more than twenty-five years old—that must have been his mother, not his wife; his brothers, not his sons—and was shirtless, revealing a boyishly flabby belly. As he came down the three front steps and approached us, I noticed his eyelashes, which were full, soft, and long, the kind of eyelashes that belong on a girl, and when placed on a boy make him look harmless. He stuck his hand out and shook the stonemason's, then smiled at me. *So this is the infamous El Muerto*, I thought. He looked about as dangerous as a piglet.

The stonemason introduced me, and I launched into my sob story, using the most polite language, the *usted* form rather than the *tu*, even though I was addressing someone who was clearly my junior in age and who, furthermore, was a known delinquent.

"I am not suggesting that you stole the computer, but perhaps you know, or could find out, who did," I said with an earnest smile. The goal here was not to get him on the defensive, but to get him on my side, and give him an out, so if he did steal it, he could be guilted into returning it with no questions asked. In essence, I was harkening back to my father, trying to let El Muerto know how hard I had been hit. I looked this young man in the eyes, which I found somewhere under all those lashes, and he looked back at me, assuring me that he was sorry about my loss and would do everything he could to help me out. His was a casual, confident denial, not contentious in the least. Then he suggested two guys who might have done it: "*El Tacho*," who lived right at the bottom of our hill; and the neighbor just across from the house, the husband of Renalda, a young man who wasn't from this town originally and so was automatically suspicious.

We repeated this scene three more times, calling out "Buenos dias" in front of a small, square home, then talking with the young man who emerged from the doorway only to deny any guilt and point the finger at someone else. El Tacho, tall, nervous, and even younger than El Muerto, fidgeted in the doorway like James Dean in *Rebel Without a Cause*. He had eyebrows shaved with a startling three-lined pattern—a gang sign, or just something he saw on MTV?—and suggested we try the husband of Renalda, who, after all, was not from here. The husband of Renalda offered up El Muerto and Julio as suspects. Julio, it turned out, was the first of the four suspects who actually looked and acted the part. Though he was the shortest of them, and probably weighed the least, he was also the scrappiest, and came out of his doorway running toward us with the ferocity of a junkyard dog.

"Do you have proof?" he wanted to know. "Because if you don't, then don't come around to my house." When the stonemason told him he'd been spotted in the vicinity of the house that was robbed, Julio responded with a jutting chest and a threatening chin. "*Es mi pueblo, y puedo ir donde quiero,*" he said: it's my town, and I can go where I want to. It was an anger I understood: I'd wanted to say the same sort of thing to the gay guys from Cleveland and Atlanta who'd sneered at me on Castro Street; to the college boy at San Francisco State who'd kicked footballs on the grass growing over our razed Gatorville homes. But it was useless to try and explain all this to a man who lived in a cinderblock house on a dirt street in a village which was being overtaken by second homes, like Casa del Sol, owned by outsiders who flew in for the week, month, or season and then flew back out.

Julio, it turned out, was also the only one of the four who believed in honor among thieves. Unlike the other suspects, he didn't try to blame anyone else, just pointed his finger at my chest and repeated emphatically, "Es mi pueblo." It's my town.

As the stonemason and I looped back to the main street, the village had quieted for the midday meal. I was hungry myself, as well as sweaty, confused, and a bit shaken, after that last encounter with Julio. The circle of suspects was now spiraling back in on itself, a never-ending Escher puzzle, and things were only murkier than they'd been two hours earlier when we'd started out on our rounds. The next day, the spiral got even tighter and more surreal: the juez told me that a rumor was circulating that the stonemason himself, known for doing drogas and familiar with the house—its doors and locks or lack thereof—was the one who had taken our stuff.

It took eight days for the police to return to start the investigation, and I spent that time annoying my hostess and everyone else in town with my relentless attempts to get the computer back; trying to improve my surfing despite my poor skills and junky second-hand board I'd lugged there from California; and hanging out with yet another older, inappropriate man who may have been a thief, of sorts, himself. It wasn't clear exactly when my hostess's attitude toward me turned from sympathy to annoyance to out-and-out hostility, but informing her that her stonemason was considered a suspect certainly did not generate any good will between us. Posting "reward" signs that invited the robbers to come back to Casa del Sol to exchange the computer for three thousand pesos only added to the breakdown of our relationship. Then, just after her other guest returned to the States, I abandoned her for a few days as well, to go on a road trip.

When an experienced surfer who has driven his four-wheel drive up and down the coast of Mexico for decades offers to take you to his "secret spot," you are no longer allowed to think of yourself as a Have Not. As we put-putted around the dirt roads on his motorbike and then in his truck, I could feel people looking at me without seeing a speck of my past, without seeing me at all, but instead seeing a mirage version of me: a tanned, fit, slightly blonde woman with a surfboard cavorting around a sea-side Mexican village with a mustachioed, slightly danger-ous American renegade. Every once in a while, a small dark wad of infinity threatened to surge up from my belly and consume me or fill me with regret or panic. But I resisted the urge to tell people who I really was. Instead, I allowed myself to become a myth, fulfilling everyone's fantasy, including my own. If I hadn't quite evolved into a Have, maybe I was now an OK, Gimme Some. I didn't care if it was truth or fiction. I didn't care where this guy got the cash to build his cliff-top house or why he could never again return to Hawaii under his own name. I just hopped on the back of his bike, paddled into the waves on my surfboard, and went along for the ride.

When I got back to Casa del Sol after the road trip, my hostess was no longer speaking to me except in terse sentences to "ask" if I would replenish the bottled water or launder the towels. Apparently, while I was gone, someone had shown up at the Casa in the middle of the night, frightening my hostess, who didn't speak Span-ish and couldn't understand what the guy, hidden in the shadows just outside her bedroom window, was saying.

But she was pretty sure it had to do with my laptop and the reward posters. She was understandably upset with me, and also afraid to spend the night in her own home, so she was now sleeping at a friend's house and returning every morning to her Casa for coffee. Now not only my estranged hostess but half the town was ignoring me. Where once they had stopped me in the street to commiserate with my tragedy, many now looked the other way. The Mexicans were just bored with the topic. "*Esta computadora debe ser muy importante a ti,*" the juez said to me finally, with a yawn and a sigh, as if to say, "Why is this damn computer so important to you, anyway?" My hostess, deigning to speak to me one morning, echoed his sentiment. "Why can't you just let it go?" she asked. And the gringo vacationers seemed to wonder the same thing: Why couldn't I accept the loss and stop reminding them of the problems that came with paradise?

So I decided to make one last-ditch effort to recover the computer, and then, I promised myself, I would let it go. First I upped the ante on my reward to five thousand pesos, about five hundred U.S. dollars, then spread the word that I would be in my room at the house, literal jail bait in my cell, with cash in hand that Thursday night to make the exchange.

The plan was to lock myself in my bedroom, stashing the key to the gate in my pillowcase, along with the reward money and my Spanish dictionary, in case I needed a word or two to help with the negotiations. I'd sleep in shorts and a T-shirt so I'd be decent when the guy showed up in the middle of the night, waking me up with a "psssst."

Then I'd sit on the end of the bed, out of his reach, and show him the cash so he knew I meant business. I'd tell him to slip the laptop case through the bars—the slats were just wide enough—and push it toward me, so I didn't have to get within touching distance of him. Then I'd open the case, plug the power cord into the outlet, to make sure it still worked and still had my life on it. There would be an awkward silence as we waited for it to boot up, and I'd be tempted to make small talk to ease the tension; plus, I never passed up a chance to practice my Spanish and learn some new local idioms. Eventually my files would appear on the screen; I'd sigh with relief, and thank him—the guy who probably stole my computer—profusely, slipping the clump of bills through the bars. I'd briefly consider negotiating with him on the reward money, or even, as a couple faux-police suggested, just plain shorting him on the cash. But I'd stick to my end of the bargain; a deal is a deal, after all, especially among thieves.

What could be dangerous? I'd be safely ensconced in my cell the whole time, and all the transactions would happen between bars. If he'd brought a weapon—a knife or a stick or one of those long, curved machetes the local men used to clear brush—he wouldn't be able to reach me with it. The only thing that could harm me was a gun, and everyone, even the people who said my plan was crazy and stupid, agreed that the criminals around here didn't have guns.

One man about my age, who had dropped out of his life back home in Southern California, was impressed by how well I'd thought it out. We were eating at the same taco stand on Thursday afternoon, and I described all the details.

"It just might work," he said, a look of goofy admiration on his face. Then he offered me a ride home on the back of his moto. And as we scaled the dirt road leading up to the Casa del Sol, I could only cross my fingers and hope that the neighbors couldn't tell the difference between one gringo on a moto and another.

SoCal wasn't the only one interested in the specifics of my plan. Later that afternoon, the Comandante, who heard about it from the juez, finally showed up to start the investigation. His plan was even more outrageous than mine: He wanted to have his assistant spend the night hiding out in the bushes by the side of the house and ambush the person who came to return the computer. But the thief obviously had his eye on the house; there was no way he'd show up if there was a cop waiting for him in the bushes. Then the Comandante wanted me to snap photos of the person who showed up to return the laptop. Had he been watching slapstick comedies along with the gangster movies? This seemed sure to foul up my chances of getting back my computer. It was just as my father had once explained to me back in Gatorville, after the police came knocking on our door: The cops were no closer to being on my side than the thieves were. In fact, their objective, which was to nab the robbers, was at odds with mine, which was to get my stuff back.

At 10:30 that night, I started my evening preparations, taking a shower to wash off the day's grime, then collecting a glass of water and a pee bucket so I wouldn't have to leave the safety of my cell all night long. Next, I rolled the reward money into a wad and stashed it, along with my weapons and Spanish dictionary, under my pillow. Then, too wasted from heat and physical exhaustion to be scared, I took my book and went to bed.

Mexican roosters have no sense of timing: They crow all night and all day, with no regard for the dawn. It was just a few days after the full moon, and the dogs and donkeys were also stirred up, while dueling disco music from distant parties wafted over as well. The night sky had an electric edge to it, and for hours I drifted in and out of sleep and something just on the edge of sleep, hazy like the smoke from the trash fires that seemed to be burning constantly. Then—I had no idea what time it was or how long I'd been adrift—out of all this haziness came a man's voice.

"Frances," it said, in a loud whisper.

I lifted my head off the pillow to make sure I wasn't dreaming.

"Frances," came the voice again.

Oh my gosh, it's him, and he knows my name, I thought, as I drifted from slightly asleep to slightly awake. "*Si, aqui.*" Yes, here, I said, in a rasping whisper to match his. Now I sat up and looked at the gate. No one was there, but footsteps were approaching.

"Aqui," I said again, and the sound of shoes on tile kept coming toward me. They lumbered along casually—apparently in Mexico, not even the thieves are in a hurry—and then they stopped, and a large figure stood in front of my gate-door, blocking the moonlight and clutching the bars. Though he faced toward me, I could not make out his features.

"I don't have your computer," he said, in English, in a distinct American accent. And then my vision came into focus on the gangly body of SoCal, dangling his arms through the bars like a monkey at the zoo and babbling apologies like an infatuated drunk, which, at that moment, he was.

"Can I come in?" he said, his voice now louder and slurring.

"Why?" I said, hoping he'd just go on his way before anyone—such as a robber with my computer—might hear him.

"You're the perfect woman. I've always loved you." His voice was no longer close to a whisper.

"You've known me for a week," I said.

"So."

He continued pleading like a puppy, and to shut him up, I finally dug the key from my pillowcase and unlocked the gate.

"That's better," he said, falling onto my bed, and proceeded to pass out.

My plan, such as it was, was ruined—no thief would be showing up after this ruckus—and now I had to figure out how to get rid of this would-be vacation lover before morning, when my hostess and my actual vacation lover might show up.

"Why can't you just let it go," my hostess had asked me a few days earlier. It was a fair question, and it came back to me in the harsh morning light, after I'd roused SoCal and sent him on his way. Was the loss of the files on the laptop so devastating? Or was it the money that it would take to replace the computer? Was I upset because the downtrodden locals didn't accept me as one of their own? Or embarrassed because I had come so far from my own downtrodden roots that I had forgotten how to protect my stuff? Would my practical older brother, who still lived in the city and was therefore fluent in the use of locks, disown me when he found out that I had "lost" something so valuable? Or was this theft simply one more downside of upward mobility: that once you have things, people can take them from you?

Maybe. But the real downside of upward mobility is that you remain poor on the inside, so even if you get money you never quite relax into it. You may travel to a third-world paradise to ride waves and motorcycles, but it will feel like it's not happening to the "true" you. And you will see yourself not only as an imposter, but also as a traitor, because you have left your family behind, your mother in a two-room studio on a noisy city street running between part-time jobs; your father in his cabin reading *National Geographic*, which he says is as satisfying for him as actually traveling. The downside is that you no longer belong with the Have Nots, but never quite take on that attitude of entitlement that comes so naturally to the true Haves and makes them, as F. Scott Fitzgerald once wrote, "different from you and me." The downside is that you become your own enemy, and not just in the sense that who you used to be would sneer at who you are now. But also in the sense that you, or rather the withered naysayer at your core, are the one sabotaging yourself, and you no longer have anyone or anything else to blame.

There were all kinds of reasons why I couldn't let that computer go. But in the end I did it anyway. I just gave up and gave in.

The day I left Mexico, in a kind of Murphy's Law for surfers, the waves got big and perfect, and I had about three hours to take advantage them. A few days earlier I'd traded in my board and a hundred dollars for a longer, rounder, better board stenciled with the profile of an American Indian in headdress, and I was eager to see what I could do with it. So I paddled out and sat up, dangling my legs in the warm Pacific and watching for the right line of swell that would rise up and crest just in front of me. My mind receded, giving in to my body, which had the superior intelligence here, and I faced those waves as if I wore blinders, oblivious to everything else around me, to past and future, to worry and loss, to ambition and disappointment, and also to all the other surfers jockeying alongside me for the waves. My attention was on those thick wedges of water heading toward me, as I put my belly to the board and paddled into their path, then popped up to my feet for the exhilarating *whoooosh* down the face of the wave. After weeks of struggling against the waves and my old board, trying too hard to incorporate some new tip, finally and suddenly, everything fell into place. I was catching every wave I paddled for, and other surfers were backing out of my way and letting me go.

I'd been out two hours when I caught a wave, popped up quick, then repositioned my feet, so I could keep the board in the upper portion, the power part, of the wave. Then, rather than glide down and out of the wave like a sophomore, I angled the board just right so it remained in that groove near the top of the crest. And then I looked in front of me and saw just how long that line of water was, and how much more wave there was to ride. So I loosened up and relaxed into it; bent my knees and swiveled my hips, leaning this way and that, swishing the board up and down the face of that wave as it opened up before me. I rode the wave all the way into the shallows, almost hitting a couple swimmers, then hopped off just before landing on the beach.

Wow, I thought. That was my best ride of this trip, maybe the best ride of my life. I loved my Indian, wanted to kiss his profile in gratitude, though I knew only part of this wow was due to the board; the other part was just magic. I also knew I should quit now, on a high note; nothing good could come from trying to replicate such grace.

But I couldn't help myself; I had to paddle out again and try for another one. And so I scooted right back out and then sat up to catch my breath and wait for my wave. When a perfect crest headed toward me, I turned around and paddled hard, felt the water lift my board from behind, popped up to my feet, and found that perfect groove where the wave seemed to be gripping my board by its own accord. Again I swiveled my hips, carved up and down, looked out to see an endless curve of water opening up in front of me. Again I rode into the shallows, almost hit a swimmer, almost beached my board, and again I stood up laughing at the impossibility of so much joy, and told myself I'd better stop right then, while I was still ahead.

And again I paddled back out and caught another wave. And for a third time I hopped to my feet, swiveled my hips, and guided the board up and down, so I was not merely walking on water, but gliding on it, dancing on it, as the wave crashed into white foam behind me, propelling me into the green, glassy water ahead. This was infinity of the brightest kind, and I slipped into that ecstasy that comes with losing yourself completely, with touching the wet fire churning at the center of the world, with getting all the way inside of life, no longer a witness but right at the crux, at the exact point of maximum propulsion. Finally the wave dropped me off at the beach, where this time I rammed my lovely Indian into the sand like an amateur and stumbled back onto land, my whole body grinning in exhaustion and elation.

Epilogue
Discover the Future of Your Past

"What do you need to sit fully into your seat?" the yoga teacher asks us in an earnest, probing voice. "To sit fully into your pose, into yourself, into your life?" she continues, as we sit on our mats and try to figure out what she's talking about. Then she instructs us to bow and "dedicate the energy of your practice" to someone. I wonder: Is dedicating my practice to someone the same thing as praying for him? I wiggle my butt on the little round meditation pillow, trying to sit fully into it, and decide to dedicate my practice to my younger brother, who has just been "transitioned" out of his job.

Dedicate, transition: every little corner of our culture has its own dialect, its own way of using words. English is a hard enough language as it is, with so many exceptions to so many rules. It makes me want to apologize to the immigrants trying to learn it, and also to my brother's daughters, ages four and six. Though born and raised in California like me, they still get tripped up by the odd conjugations and pronunciations of their native tongue: Why, for instance, we say we *caught* something instead of we *catched* it. And why we pronounce *Ford* one way and *word* another. "I'm sorry," I want to say to my nieces, to the children I tutor in the San Francisco schools, to the Mexicans I meet in the dressing room at Mervyn's, to all students of English, both native and foreign-born. This language makes little sense. Even the sound of it is harsh, unlike Spanish, which jangles like oversized earrings.

"I got transitioned out of my job," my younger brother tells me in a soft, sad voice. He's speaking English, but I don't understand what he means until he explains that "transitioned" is a fancy way of saying "fired" or, as in his case, "laid off." His name means "he who laughs," and he usually lives up to it. His is a sweet giggle that can be endearing coming from a big, sports-loving, meat-eating guy like him. He also cries more than any other man I have ever met. And that, too, in a man his size, is endearing, and also heartbreaking, especially since I'm his older sister and our "family of origin," as the social workers call it, was poor and divorced, we children evicted too early from our one and only childhood. I want to give my brother a severance check and a gold watch—everything that his company, a local television station, did not give him. While I'm at it, I want to give him parents who attended his high school football games, a car for his sixteenth birthday, and introductions to a couple of sports-media personalities who could, with a phone call, set him up with fifty thousand dollars a year and video equipment to produce his own local sports program.

My brother's six-year-old daughter is named Mille— pronounced "Millie." Her first-grade teacher has taught her about silent *e*'s, but her name, she and I realize one day while she's practicing her reading at the kitchen table, has the opposite of a silent *e*. What would that be? A noisy *e*? A loud-and-proud *e*? Mille's sister, two years younger and always wanting to keep up, tells me she can write her name as well. She just throws down those letters—and she's got a lot of them in Tallulah—onto the paper. She doesn't care what order they're in: that's her name. She is at the age when she does not understand the difference between fact and opinion, between knowing something to be true and wanting it to be so. Like certain politicians and talk-show hosts, she operates under a paradigm of conviction: If she feels strongly enough about something, it must be right.

"Saturn is the biggest planet on Earth," she told me the other day, as if daring me to contradict her.

"I don't know about that," I said, taking her bait.

"Yes, it is," she said, not a trace of doubt in her voice, as if she were saying, *I like strawberry yogurt best.*

I appreciate her boldness, and I respond with a giggle that sounds like her father's, he who laughs. This kind of conviction can be endearing in a four-year-old, though not so endearing in a talk-show host, nor in the president of a country—people who hold the fate of so many lives in that slender gap between their confidence and their ignorance. But perhaps my niece is just discovering the delicious power of proclaiming what you believe to be true about the universe, whether it be about Saturn's relationship to Earth, or—as with her aunt's proclamations—about poverty's relationship to the soul.

—

The first thing I need in order to sit fully into my seat is a better chair. Everything I own I've scrounged, so none of it necessarily fits the purpose to which I've put it. I grew up poor, and I still don't know which verb tense—past or present—to use between the subject *I* and the adjective *poor*. But no matter how much money I'm pulling in, it just doesn't seem right to buy something brand-new and designed for only one function: like, say, a chair to use at a computer.

You don't have to be poor to cultivate this habit of buying secondhand or doubling and tripling up on the uses of things; you could also be an environmentalist. But those of us who reduce, reuse, and recycle out of necessity can sometimes have trouble spending money on something costly that we really need, even if we could maybe afford it. We live in fear of becoming poor in the future, like we were in the past, and maybe even are in the present. But that doesn't keep us from wanting: Wanting that office chair covered in breathable blue, red, or black nylon with the adjustable seat and padded back. Wanting this thing so badly because we believe that if we get it, it will help us achieve everything we've ever dreamed of doing or having or being.

Truth be told, though, what I really want is that cool Eames-style task chair with the ergonomic design that relieves neck, back, and shoulder pain; the one that comes in muted tones of burnt orange and pale puke green and has levers for shifting back and forth, up and down, and around and around. Then I'd be sitting pretty. Then I'd be sitting fully into my seat. Then I'd be wheeling around my desk, watching my fingers buzz along the keyboard; seeing the words and sentences blossom onto the electronic screen; letting the answering machine take my calls from nine to one every day, because those are my creative hours; and returning those calls only after I did my yoga and had my lunch of crab and avocados (if they were in season) and organic baby arugula dressed in a locally grown Meyer-lemon vinaigrette.

Not everyone who grows up poor is infected by such an audacious imagination. My older brother, for instance, succumbed to cynicism instead of escapism, spending years at a union job laying carpeting and hanging signs rather than trying to find work with plants or children or other things that made him happy. Though he did, in his forties, become a teacher and a husband and a step-father; so perhaps that cynicism succumbed, finally, to him. But when I was a girl, I escaped into that dream of the loudspeaker picking me out of the crowd on the corner of 16th and Sanchez, with the helicopter sending down a rope ladder and then transporting me to the Paris-salon-in-the-clouds where I really belonged, where everything would finally be perfect. My life would be (conditional tense, describing the future of my past) my art: writing, filmmaking, whatever. My younger brother's conditional life would be sports: first playing them, then reporting them on television, plus a little acting in movies and TV commercials on the side. It would be the O.J. Simpson trajectory. This was before O.J. became a joke about a glove and a white Bronco, back when he was a star athlete who came from an even worse neighborhood in San Francisco than we did.

"There's the way you talk, and there's the way you write," I tell the kids I tutor in the crowded public schools of inner-city San Francisco. (Of course, *crowded*, *public*, and *inner-city* are code for mostly poor and not white.) I don't want them to turn their backs on their way of talking, because they need it to stay tethered to themselves, to maintain an address in their neighborhoods so they'll always have a place to call home. But I also want to teach these kids the language of school, jobs, money, and power; of filling out forms and applications and making reports and statements to the press. They need to learn this breakable and breaking and broken language of English, with its many coded ways to say one thing and mean another: The yoga code, in which we aim to "sit fully into our seats." The business code, in which people get "transitioned" out of their jobs, and out of their dreams as well. The code of doctors, who have words that allow them to speak of sickness and dying without falling apart. The code of secretaries, who return your question (*Is the boss in?*) with one of their own (*Who's calling?*).

The organization where I volunteer sometimes sends me into classrooms, and other times I meet with students at the tutoring center, which happens to be located on a sooty, Spanish-speaking street a few blocks down and over from the one on which I grew up. I attended an editorial meeting at this center with a half-dozen volunteer tutors and a dozen high school students, whom we were

helping to produce a book of oral histories. A big topic
of discussion—especially among the adults—was how
much we should change the wording of these oral histories in order to make them accessible to readers. The
students had conducted their interviews in many different languages: in English and Spanish and street English
and Spanglish; in rural Southern and urban Northern; in
Tagalog pure and Tagalog second-generation; in Samoan,
Mandarin, Cantonese, Vietnamese, Khmer, Thai, and Lao-
tian; in the many dialects of islands and wars and cities, of
ambition and survival and remembering and forgetting.

Finally one boy pointed out that he and his fellow
students had to take classes to understand certain books,
because the authors—guys named Twain and Shakespeare—wrote in ways that were inaccessible to many
readers. "If we have to study *them* to understand *their*
writing," he wondered, "why shouldn't people have to
study *us* to understand *our* writing?" We, the adults, were
silent. It was a brilliant question. No one had an answer.

But there is an answer: You've got to write right—i.e.,
white—in order to get ahead. At the same time, you can't
desert your natural way of speaking and writing, which
is also your way of thinking and eating and sleeping, of
fighting and kissing and dreaming, because you can't
burn down your own home. You've got to learn at least
two languages: one to make it out of the neighborhood,
and one to keep a foothold in it.

When you volunteer, people assume you are well-off:
Who else but the rich could afford to work for free? Even

the people working with you at the tutoring organization assume you fit into the category of financially *comfortable*, a term that makes it sound as if money were a fluffy bathrobe or a pair of slippers. This assumption is made even if you are (or once were, and maybe one day will again be) poor. Even if you are volunteering because you are bereft and looking for human interactions that go beyond "Next in line" and "Will that be all for you today?" Even if you just want a reason to return to the rowdy streets you knew as a child, streets filled with yelling and yearning, with people making do and making art and making catcalls at you. Even if you just want to help arm these kids—who are your peers, except thirty years younger—with the munitions of language, the native speakers and the English-language learners alike. You know (present) from experience (past) that they will need (future) an arsenal of words and phrases and paragraphs in order to maybe get somewhere in a world that employs this complicated, breakable English language. You also know, also from experience, how lonely it is to be stranded in that world without a place that feels like home.

In white parlance, *urban* is code for poor and non-white, which in San Francisco usually means black or Mexican. *Mexican* itself is really just shorthand for a native of any Central or South American country, and sometimes even of Guam, Samoa, and the Philippines. There are many Chinese students in the city's urban neighborhoods, but they generally don't get classified as "urban" unless they're members of a gang. The newer and less-accomplished Asian immigrants, however, from countries such as Vietnam or Laos, are often called "urban," though they are generally the most rural of us all, searching for something that feels like soil underneath all this pavement. The rich (white) people in this city live at the tops of hills, while the poor (nonwhites) live at the bottoms. You can be a city dweller all your life, but if you live at the top of an asphalt hill rather than in a valley, you will never be considered "urban."

Also, the hilltops, and even the neighborhoods on the inclines, have a special parking system that works by code. If you speak the language and can afford to live in the neighborhood, you get a permit to prove it and can park wherever you want for however long. In the valleys and urban neighborhoods, however, parking is a free-for-all. This helps facilitate a kind of one-way tourism in which rich white people can travel at will into the lower, louder neighborhoods, buy a burrito and a cheap beer or maybe a bag of drugs, then drive safely back to their comfortable homes and ease into their robes and slippers. But the opposite is not so easily accomplished, thus helping to keep the riffraff sequestered in the valleys. (Most of us would rather be there anyway, because not only is it foggier on those bayside hills, but it's too damn quiet as well.)

If you're that rare combination of white *and* urban, you present a classification problem—unless you are a *punk*, which is a person who is poor on purpose; or an *artist*, which is a punk with a purpose; or *white trash*, which is certainly not something anyone is on purpose. But if you are white and educated and dress nicely, people are going to assume you are not urban. Other white people at the organization where you volunteer are going to assume you're from the heights or the suburbs or a nice two-parent home back east or up north.

The fact is, if you're going to be white in this type of hip arts organization, you've got to dress down and a little geeky in order to be taken seriously. You've got to look like you're part of the group I've come to call the *grungerati*—writers and painters and performers who apparently feel it would be selling out to buy clothes that match or a sexy pair of shoes. You've got to wear unflattering cat's-eye or rectangular glasses and dress in oversaturated, disagreeable colors, like burnt orange and pale puke green. Plaids with stripes are appropriate, and thick, colored tights if you're female, or a wrinkled madras shirt if you're male. Very important: Do not iron your clothes. Even mending is frowned upon.

But let's say you happen to have dressed in this manner as a child in this very neighborhood in the 1970s, because your parents could not afford new clothes or keep up with ironing, and when you outgrew your dresses, your mother had you wear them over pants, as if they had suddenly become blouses. You may then have spent a lifetime coveting clothes that fit, that look new and sharp, as opposed to reused and recycled. You may have learned how to look nice without spending a lot of money. You may have adopted a certain urban style: sleek, closefitting, a little flashy. Rich and middle-class white folks might think it's tacky, but at least it's put together—no holes; no wrinkles; no big, fat, ugly shoes.

When I go on a tutoring assignment in the schools—

the same schools my brothers and I once attended—the students compliment me on my clothes. "She dress good for a old person," one girl says, pointing to me. Their mothers understand me, too. We nod almost imperceptibly to each other. We're single women trying to get ahead and stay ahead. We've got to look good, take life seriously, be ready at all times to jump on an opportunity or avoid a rip-off or find someone to watch the kids if a date or a job interview comes up. My co-workers at the tutoring organization, who generally share my skin tone and hair texture, speak to me in polite code, feigning respect while simultaneously dissing me. Mothers who come in dressed like me get the bright, over-the-top smiles of the privileged to the underprivileged, or the advantaged to the disadvantaged, or however the social workers are putting it these days. I confound everybody: light hair, green eyes, tight blouse, big earrings, pants with flair and no wrinkles, talking about novelist Jamaica Kincaid's economy of language and also conversing in Spanish about where to get avocados on sale five for a dollar, not too bruised.

"What are you?" a white woman asked me recently. It's a question I have heard in various forms throughout my life. "Are you black?" a young woman, whose parents were from India, wanted to know after I got off the dance floor. "Are you Brazilian?" a black semipro basketball player asked me after a game. "*De dónde eres?* (Where are you from?) the Mexicans ask when I speak to them in their language, which I heard everywhere while growing up, wandering the streets of my neighborhood bored, lonely, and curious. Tantalized by this foreign tongue and wanting to break its secret code, I studied and practiced Spanish for years. And though I speak it with an accent that can fool even native speakers, it is still not anything I can call my own. Which reminds me: What I need besides a chair is a house and a family and a city and a language to which I belong.

I once tutored students at a private college in New England. (It was my job; I wasn't volunteering for free.) Of course, *private college* and *New England* are code words for white and well-off, or at least comfortable. I'm pretty sure the students all had robes and slippers. But even these kids, whose primary language was English, had trouble transitioning (if I may borrow the term from my brother's former employer) from speaking English to writing it. I'd have them read their papers aloud to me so we could hear the words in neutral airspace, as if encountering them for the first time. Their voices would drop into a formal octave to pronounce the long, convoluted sentences fortified by the thesaurus and held together by the authority vested in the passive voice. These students tripped and fell over their own words. After a paragraph or two I came to their rescue, stopping them with a gentle tap on the arm so they didn't have to suffer anymore.

"What I *meant* was," they'd say to me, falling back into their normal speaking tone and everyday subject-verb-object constructions. And then they'd explain in a few clear words what they had been trying to say in the awkward, formal language of college essays and official documents.

As a tutor in San Francisco's public schools, I have read this same impenetrable language on school assignments handed out by teachers. I have sat next to eleven-, fourteen-, and sixteen-year-olds who wanted to know what this written assignment was asking them to do, and I have frequently been unable to answer them. Reading those sheets is like being lost in France: a few words sound familiar, but I have no idea how they are connected to one another, or to me. When I was a student in these same classrooms, I often felt this same bewilderment, but I always assumed it was I who was illiterate, and that the language of academia was correct. Now I feel like a social worker advocating for clarity. I keep wanting to ask the teachers, "But what do you *mean*?" and see if they, like the New England college students I once tutored, can translate their prose into words that make sense.

The students in the city's public schools, meanwhile, may not be fluent in the convoluted English of official written papers, but they sure know how to fly back and forth among several other languages. One teenage girl, half Mexican and half Filipina, glides between Spanish, Tagalog, and English, creating an *idioma* of her own. Snapping her gum, she takes a surreptitious peek at her cellphone, glances at the assignment sheet, and says to me, "Chica, what I'm supposed to do here?"

To get to the volunteer center, you must pass through a storefront that has been turned into a gift shop to help fund the tutoring program. It resembles a museum gift shop, except it's dark and overstuffed, almost as if it were designed to confuse people who come in off the street, blinking their eyes to adjust to the dim light and wondering where they've landed. For some reason the gift shop has a pirate theme, and so, along with books and T-shirts, it also sells eye patches, skull-and-crossbones flags, treasure maps, and other "pirate supplies." And, on the floor at the far end of the counter, perhaps most confounding of all, is a large barrel of lard.

Apparently lard is some kind of pirate thing. And apparently *pirate*, in a language I don't understand, is some kind of writer thing, or maybe a rebel thing, or a grungerati thing. (Like I said, I don't speak this language.) There is a store log—counterpart, I suppose, to a ship's log—and people write in it about the lard: reminiscences, appreciations, facts about lard, or at least beliefs they feel strongly to be true. The lard barrel is a source of many nervous laughs and quizzical looks, and also knowing smirks from a certain demographic that finds profound irony in that tub. The lard is not actually sold, but you can barter for it. I'm not sure what the store takes in trade for a lump, a lick, a pound of the stuff. How do you measure out lard from a barrel? By the scoop? The handful? The bootful? And what do you keep it in once you get it home? These are the kinds of questions the lard inspires, and perhaps this is its reason for being in a wooden keg in the shop that fronts the room where tutors and students work together on writing sentences and stories: It's there to ignite surprise, to arouse curiosity, to explore the slippery terrain between confusion and understanding.

I think the lard serves another purpose as well: It acts

as a litmus test for distinguishing the people who "get" the lard—or act as if they do—from the people who don't. For the Spanish-speaking moms and kids who live in the neighborhood and walk past the keg to get to their tutoring sessions, lard is not an ironic joke; it's food. They use it to make *refritos*, to fry *rellenas*, to get their calories to fuel their bodies. But in the pirate store, it sits in an open-mouthed wooden keg, collecting grime like a New York City snowbank. Splotches of lard spill out of the keg and smear themselves on nearby shelves, books, cards, and other items. A middle-aged man walks by in a button-up shirt and nice, creased slacks. His pleats flirt with a tuft of lard sticking out of the keg like frosting. Somehow he strolls by without noticing how close he came to getting greased.

My gut feeling is that lard stains do not come out of clothes easily, if at all, though I do not know this to be a fact. I only feel it strongly to be true, the way my four-year-old niece knows that Saturn is the biggest planet on Earth. My gut feeling is that the neighborhood moms who launder and iron the clothes of their sons and daughters do not get the joke of the lard and would prefer their children not stick their hands into the tub and then, as children will do, touch those lard-dipped hands to their shirts, dresses, jackets, hair, and faces.

Perhaps it is because I come from this neighborhood, or perhaps it is because I moved away, but I tend to worry about these children, about all children. How will they ever learn enough to be successful, and how will they ever *un*learn enough to be happy? Yet they proceed undaunted, or perhaps unaware of the sheer amount of information—both facts and opinions, often conflicting—that lies in wait, ready to ambush them.

"Hey," says my niece with the unsilent *e*, "the word *eye* is pronounced the same as the word *I*…but they don't have any of the same letters." She is delighted with her cleverness at having made this discovery, and with the cleverness of the English language, the way it doesn't make sense but still seems to make sense anyway. We are sitting at the kitchen table doing homework out of a purple folder. And though she is actually on her knees in the chair—her legs folded underneath her, the soles of her bare feet facing up, her bottom resting on her calves—she is sitting fully into her seat. Next to her, perched on the edge of my own chair, I try to figure out if my time has passed, if I have both absorbed and lost too much to ever get my body to unfurl like that again, or if I still might have a chance to settle into my own place in this world.

ACKNOWLEDGEMENTS

First and foremost I thank my family for everything they have given me, including the freedom to write a book which tells only one side of the story. Thanks in particular to my mother for passing her love of the written word on to me; my father for showing me what it means to be a craftsman; and my brothers for the support and the teasing.

I also offer my gratitude to:

Publisher and editor Pat Walsh and agent Amy Rennert for believing in this book from the very beginning and seeing it all the way through; editor Robyn Russell for her sharp eye and soft voice; The best writing group in the world, Ann Harleman (who first encouraged me to write about my own life), Gail Donovan, and Elizabeth Searle; Sy Safransky, Andrew Snee, Colleen Donfield, Tim McKee, and the rest of the staff at *The Sun* magazine for first publishing the essays that would eventually become this book; readers who offered crucial feedback on versions of the manuscript, including book midwife Caroline Pincus, Kirsten Platt, Gillian Kendall, Yanina Gotulsky, and James Warner; The Hedgebrook writing retreat, where I first began piecing this book together; friends and supporters from way back, including Jack Reich, Kathi Gemma, Dick Reed, Spencer Billings, Martha Bebinger, Rachel Buff, Brian Winn, Mike Stone, Rachel Phipps, John Costin, Jane Murphy, Terry Murphy, Tasha Fulkerson, and Delia Maroney; the skeleton crew at MacAdam/Cage, including designer Dorothy Carico Smith (who created the captivating cover), Guy Intoci, and Michelle Dotter.

A final thanks to anyone over the years who ever put me up or got me in for free or just nodded in encouragement.